UNIVERSITY OF NORTH CAROLINA AT CHAPEL HILL
DEPARTMENT OF ROMANCE LANGUAGES

NORTH CAROLINA STUDIES
IN THE ROMANCE LANGUAGES AND LITERATURES

Founder: URBAN TIGNER HOLMES
Editor: CAROL L. SHERMAN

Distributed by:

UNIVERSITY OF NORTH CAROLINA PRESS

CHAPEL HILL
North Carolina 27515-2288
U.S.A.

NORTH CAROLINA STUDIES IN THE
ROMANCE LANGUAGES AND LITERATURES
Number 258

THE RAVISHMENT OF PERSEPHONE

THE RAVISHMENT OF PERSEPHONE

Epistolary Lyric in the
Siècle des Lumières

BY

JULIA K. DE PREE

CHAPEL HILL

NORTH CAROLINA STUDIES IN THE ROMANCE
LANGUAGES AND LITERATURES
U.N.C. DEPARTMENT OF ROMANCE LANGUAGES

1998

Library of Congress Cataloging-in-Publication Data

De Pree, Julia Knowlton.
  The ravishment of Persephone: epistolary lyric in the Siècle des Lumières / by Julia K. De Pree.

  p. – cm. – (North Carolina studies in the Romance languages and literatures; no. 258)
  Includes bibliographical references and index
  ISBN 0-8078-9262-9 (pbk.)
  1. Epistolary fiction, French – History and criticism. 2. French prose literature – 18th century – History and criticism. 3. French prose literature – Women authors – History and criticism. I. Title. II. Series.

PQ637.E6D4 1998
843'.5099287 – dc21   98-34186
                                                                                        CIP

Cover design: Shelley Greundler

© 1998. Department of Romance Languages. The University of North Carolina at Chapel Hill.

ISBN 0-8078-9262-9

DEPÓSITO LEGAL: V. 3.709 - 1998

ARTES GRÁFICAS SOLER, S. A. - LA OLIVERETA, 28 - 46018 VALENCIA

TABLE OF CONTENTS

	Page
INTRODUCTION	11
PRELUDE: THE RAVISHMENT OF PERSEPHONE	21

PART I: STRUCTURES IN EPISTOLARY LYRIC

CH. 1: *L'ECHANGE UNILATÉRAL:* SOLITUDE	43
CH. 2: BLANK SPACE AND THE EPISTOLARY *HORS-SCÈNE*	54
CH. 3: THE SHORT TEXT: *INACHÈVEMENT*	66

PART II: THEMES IN EPISTOLARY LYRIC

CH. 4: WRITING AS MOURNING: SUBSTITUTIONS OF PRESENCE IN RICCOBONI'S *LETTRES DE MISTRESS FANNI BUTLERD*	81
CH. 5: DIVERSIONS OF DESIRE: *LETTRES DE MILADY JULIETTE CATESBY À MILADY HENRIETTE CAMPLEY, SON AMIE*	103
CH. 6: MEDIATING DESIRE: THE VEIL IN *LA NOUVELLE HÉLOÏSE* AND IN *LETTRES DE MISTRESS FANNI BUTLERD*	131
POSTLUDE: WINTER INTO SPRING	154
BIBLIOGRAPHY	159

to
CGD and CLS,
always,

and to
my daughters
Claire and Madeleine

L'art ne fait que des vers; le coeur seul est poète.
                                                ANDRÉ CHÉNIER

INTRODUCTION

This study questions the notion that in the French tradition, the eighteenth century was a *siècle sans poésie*. My interest in nuancing the misleading concept of a lyric *void* stems from my graduate training, during which time required readings stressed the idea that aside from Chénier, the eighteenth century was a time in which lyric purpose was eclipsed by epistemological and philosophical discourses. As I read and studied the texts that have traditionally comprised the literary canon of the Enlightenment–in particular Rousseau's *Nouvelle Héloïse* and *Rêveries*–it seemed clear to me that the Lyric had taken refuge in prose.[1] When I later encountered and studied the epistolary texts of Graffigny, Riccoboni, and Charrière, a theory of epistolary lyric began to take shape in my mind. Epistolary lyric, it occurred to me, formed a kind of bridge between the seventeenth-century poetic text (written in the stately *alexandrin*) and the plural, revolutionary poetic forms of nineteenth-century France, including the prose poem. As a theoretical bridge, this view describes lyric continuity over time rather than emphasizing chronological disintegration or rupture.

---

[1] In her book *Le Poème en prose de Baudelaire jusqu'à nos jours*, Suzanne Bernard posits Rousseau as one of the earliest influences on the development of the prose poem. Roger Little has affirmed the importance of the eighteenth century on the development of the prose poem by bringing to light three prose poems written by Saint-Lambert, and by reiterating that "on n'hésite pas, au siècle des Lumières, tant en anglais qu'en français d'ailleurs, à appliquer le terme de poème en prose à ce que nous appelons communément roman aujourd'hui" (113). In Chapter Three I argue that the hybrid nature of epistolary writing lends itself to the designation of prose poetry.

In speaking of epistolary lyric as a bridge form I am concerned primarily with the evolution *away* from the Classical esthetic (typified in Racine) and *toward* the early Romantic sensibility (typified in Rousseau). I am therefore generally concerned with the period of roughly 1650-1800, although my primary analyses of individual epistolary texts are all situated in the eighteenth century. As with all generalizations, the terms Classical and Romantic may easily be deconstructed and shown to be faulty: Racine's verses express a certain Romanticism, and Romantic poets such as Hugo and Lamartine continued to employ the alexandrine line of verse. Nevertheless, it is at times helpful to refer to *general* designations of literary periods in discussing the evolution of Lyric in the eighteenth century, if only to show how epistolary writing resists generic categorization. My specific interest lies in showing how the epistolary prose writer *recuperated* lyric purpose from a poetic form–the alexandrine–that had become too restrictive. As I shall demonstrate in Chapter Two, epistolary lyric evolves in part from the dramatic art of Racine; as such it shares a relation with the Classical esthetic based on contiguity in time.

My interest in shaping a view of chronological continuity within the French tradition leads me to focus on the ways in which epistolary writers adopted and blended disparate elements from the late seventeenth century. Many epistolary writers employ the character of the confidante, as Janet Altman has suggested in *Epistolarity*, and individual authors such Riccoboni also adopt specific strategies such as the *deus ex machina*, as I show in Chapter Five. The epistolary vogue may be seen as an evolution *out* of the late seventeenth-century esthetic, and it is this evolution that constitutes the focus of this study. The concept of the Baroque, which has been debated at great length, does not figure prominently into my theoretical framework; rather, I undertake to describe the complexities of an esthetic coming *out* of Classicism and not, as others have done, those of Classicism itself.[2] My efforts lie in articulating the esthetic strategies

---

[2] E.B.O. Borgerhoff has considered the complicated tensions within and between French Baroque and French Classicism, concluding that the fundamental idea of Classicism is that of "true classic balance" between an affective awareness and an intellectual awareness on the part of the writer (238, 240). The "complex of Classicism," as he sees it, is a function of this balance that is always ready to come undone. The beauty of the Classical era, he further writes, is that "the century seems completely lacking in the kind of self-consciousness with respect to its artistic

by which writers—in particular women writers—eschewed the confines of what Joan DeJean has called the "classic, eternal values" theorized by Boileau and put into practice by Racine (*TG* 166).³ It is precisely the supposed *lack* of favor for lyric poetry that coincided with the latter half of the seventeenth century that interests me: I call this formal refusal of personal expression the ravishment of Lyric. Throughout the present study I shall argue that what followed this ravishment was not, as many have asserted, a period of lyric dormancy. Rather, the lyric *je* renewed itself in epistolary prose, due mainly to the recuperative gesture of the *épistolière*.

What is epistolary lyric? According to the definitions and illustrations that I provide in this study, it may be defined in its very broadest sense as the inscription of first-person experience—or *je*—in prose. Where there is a *je*, I argue, there is Lyric, regardless of distinctions between verse and prose.⁴ Monophonic, epistolary writing—wherein a *je* writes to no one or to an absent *tu*—stages the intimate yet solitary drama of the lyric voice. The simplicity of this form—letter after letter with no trace of response—belies a complexity that is its hallmark. This complexity has to do with the attempt to create presence on the page while simultaneously affirming a separation in time and space. The alternation of words and blank space depicts this complex gesture of communication within a state of absence.

---

mission which we have come to expect from our artists. It did not feel the necessity of choosing" (241).

Jean-Pierre Chauveau further elucidates the complexities of seventeenth-century esthetics when he writes that "ces 'universeaux' [baroque, classique] n'avaient guère de réalité dans la conscience des hommes du XVIIe siècle...." (10).

³ In Chapter Five of *Tender Geographies*, DeJean reiterates the enormous and regrettable impact of Boileau on all French writers, and in particular on women writers. She describes the literary battle between Boileau, who condemned the novel, and Huet, who saw in the novel "a genre that takes advantage of permeable frontiers" (175). DeJean emphasizes the fact that Boileau's influence won out over Huet's, and submits that Boileau's attack on the novel was in large part due "to the fact that the most successful first novelists were women" (181). In emphasizing the ways in which epistolary writing *resists* the legacy of Boileau, I am attempting to delineate a theory of epistolary lyric as a postclassical esthetic strategy.

⁴ It is in this context that twentieth-century readers have written effortlessly on the poetics of Proust, or the lyric voice in Duras. By the twentieth century, following the poetic revolutions of Symbolism and Surrealism, prose lyric had become freed from its moorings. In the eighteenth century, this kind of prose lyric was beginning to emerge, but continued to be hampered by codified views of generic categorization.

Confirming what has been accepted as the general view of the eighteenth-century over time, Jean-Pierre Chauveau writes of "un XVIIIe siècle qui triomphe quasi exclusivement, du moins aux yeux de la postérité, dans la *prose*" (10 my emphasis). My purpose in this study of epistolary lyric is to show that while the line of verse may have all but disappeared in the eighteenth century, lyric expression did not. Rather, I maintain, it was subverted–ravished–only to be renewed and remade in epistolary prose.

Myth provides me with an allegorical framework for illustrating this notion. The myth of Persephone dramatizes a death and a rebirth, and I use the story to illustrate the fate of Lyric in early modern France. The Persephone story also captures something of the fate of women writers during this period, for as Joan DeJean has shown, the late seventeenth century saw the categorical exclusion of almost all women writers from the original process of canon formation (*TG* 13). This suppression of the female voice may be read as a ravishment not unlike that of the lyric, and it remained the grounding gesture of the French canon. Nevertheless, by the mid-eighteenth century, women writers such as Graffigny and Riccoboni enjoyed a degree of financial success and public respect: thus was the woman writer reborn after the cultural death imposed by the "absolute literary authority" of Boileau (DeJean *TG* 164). Like Lyric itself, I shall argue, the woman writer and the female characters she creates undergo a process of eclipse and reappearance, but they are never completely undone. Because it is a preeminent tale of alternation between disappearance and reappearance, the myth of Persephone illustrates the fluctuating fate over time of both Lyric and the woman writer.

What are the formal structures of epistolary lyric? In Part One of this book I discuss three defining structures that elucidate the term: the unilateral exchange, repetitive blank space, and brevity. The unilateral exchange characterizes all of the primary texts that I have chosen to discuss: Graffigny's *Lettres d'une Péruvienne* (1747), Riccoboni's *Lettres de Mistress Fanni Butlerd* (1757) and *Lettres de Milady Juliette Catesby à Henriette Campley, son amie* (1759), and Charrière's *Lettres de Mistress Henley* (1784). The *mise-en-scène du je* of the monophonic register emphasizes a solitary inscription of the personal in the absence of the Other; it is in this sense that it constitutes lyric expression. Through a reading of solitude in Graffigny's text, I ascertain in Chapter One the predominantly lyric quality of what Rousset has called "un duo dont on n'entend qu'une voix" (FS 78).

In Chapter Two I discuss the importance of blank space within the esthetic framework of epistolary lyric. Still in the context of Graffigny's *Lettres d'une Péruvienne*, I argue that *le blanc* influences the ways in which readers apprehend epistolary prose insofar as it effects ruptures or gaps with respect to narrative continuity. Building on the scholarship of Janet Altman and of Elizabeth Goldsmith, I link epistolary writing with dramatic writing of the seventeenth century. As an evolution in prose of the dramatic *hors-scène*, I show how blank space becomes in the epistolary text the space of unseen action and untold emotion. Because it announces an absence and a space beyond language, blank space relates profoundly to Lyric and may be read in Lacanian terms as a mute flag or emblem of the unconscious.

Brevity is the third formal element that I describe as being pertinent to epistolary lyric. Epistolary texts such as Charrière's *Mistress Henley* (and including Guilleragues's *Lettres portugaises*) are unique by virtue of their notably short length. Brevity cultivates open-endedness; both are aligned with lyric purpose. The *short* epistolary text therefore differs from the lengthier novel and as such does not readily adhere to certain conventions of novelistic form, such as linear plot progression or narrative closure. Personal (if fictive) letters that encode rhetorical figures and pleasing tonalities within language may in addition be associated with the history of the French prose poem. By calling the short texts novels, today's readers may miss the esthetic import of openness and brevity. Readers might instead consider the term *letter text* as one that encompasses greater esthetic possibilities. As Joan DeJean points out, "terminological innovation" arose during the time of Lafayette to provide inventive generic markers for uniquely female literary forms (*TG* 227). Current scholarship stands to benefit from a renewed practice of terminological innovation.

In Part Two I relate the predominant theme of epistolary writing to the formal lyric elements that I described in Part One. This form of writing most often expresses the idea of desire as it relates to absence. Epistolary writing, perhaps more than dramatic or conventional (third-person) novelistic writing, revisits almost incessantly the theme of desire in relation to absence—of a longed-for person or reply. Moreover, it stages the failure of language to reinstate presence while suggesting a certain pleasure in the attempt. Citing examples such as Saint-Preux's possessive anxiety with regard to Julie's portrait (Letter 22, Book II) as well as Fanni Butlerd's fetishism of written correspondence, I show how the epistolary exchange insists upon the role of the letter as a substitution or go-between among bodies, minds, and hearts. As such, epistolary writing emphasizes a separated union wherein writing traces the path of a desire that can be realized only in the absence of the other.

Chapter Four describes the ways in which epistolary writing compensates for the failure of presence⁵ through the operation of substitution. Through a reading of Riccoboni's *Lettres de Mistress Fanni Butlerd*, I show how writing allows the protagonist to reconcile herself to the double loss of brother (lost to death) and lover (lost through betrayal). The acts of preservation and memorialization that Fanni performs in writing letters allow her to move through loss to attain what I call a kind of lonely enlightenment. The solitude embraced by Fanni at the outcome of this process of substitution is tied in to the monophonic form chosen by Riccoboni: both form and content insist on the force of solitude as the final expression of desire.

In Chapter Five I continue my discussion of Marie-Jeanne Riccoboni by contrasting the melancholic process of writing as substitution with the notion of desire as diversion. In *Lettres de Milady Juliette Catesby à Milady Henriette Campley, son amie*, desire again emerges as a dialectic between absence and presence; however, this time the dialectic becomes a light-hearted game. The protagonist

---

⁵ In this Introduction and throughout this study, I employ the expressions failure of presence, anxiety of presence, and disappearance of presence. They are roughly analogous to each other with the exception that the third expression applies to a specifically Lacanian context. The idea of presence as *inquiétude* or failure comes out of the primary texts I discuss. Saint-Preux's famous opening line—"il faut vous fuir, mademoiselle"—summarizes the anxiety that accompanies physical contact or union. In the context of Enlightenment thought, presence fails because it grounds the subject in the real and prevents access to the ideal. As such, presence obstructs communion. This theme is depicted even before the Enlightenment, in Mme de Lafayette's famous rendering of the Princess of Clèves who prefers the memorializing gaze over physical touch.

The expression *disappearance of presence* has more to do with a Lacanian reading insofar as Lacan posits an initial plenitude of presence before the subject's fall into language. For Lacan, existence in language is irrevocably inferior to the unknowable perfection of first presence. All that remains, Lacan implies, is a shadowy awareness or remembrance: imagination.

Juliette plays out her conflict between personal honor and desire by donning the mask of writing. From behind this mask—the letters she sends to her confidante and mirror Henriette—Juliette comes to know the truth of her desire. The thematic emphasis on masking, diversion, and play are associated with the literary rococo, as I point out in this chapter; this rather playful treatment on the part of Riccoboni demonstrates the agility with which she moves from one literary register to another. Though the theme is played out very differently from her first text, *Juliette Catesby* recapitulates the ultimate theme of lyric writing: desire as absence.

The veil figures most eloquently this ultimate theme, and in Chapter Six I undertake a comparison of veil-imagery in Rousseau's *Julie, ou la nouvelle Héloïse* and in Riccoboni's *Lettres de Mistress Fanni Butlerd*. The veil underscores much of the esthetic in Rousseau's text, since it is the visual emblem of the anxiety of presence. Julie's own desires remain veiled in her life, and her body is religiously veiled in death so that those who desire *her*—Saint-Preux, Wolmar, Claire—may be spared the empty center of their quest. The veil, in other words, mediates between bodily reality and the dreamer's desire. As such, it may be read as the visual equivalent to the letter: both obey an esthetic of distancing that allows the subject to cultivate an illusion of presence. Yet while Rousseau's text implies that this illusion is superior to the broken knowledge of desire, Riccoboni's depicts a female protagonist who *removes* the veil of illusion to face the ultimate vanity of desire for another. Through the strategy of unveiling, I argue, Fanni Butlerd emerges as an antithesis to Rousseau's Julie, since she chooses an imperfect, unveiled life over the perfection of death.

Desire as absence, the anxiety of presence, the letter as negotiator between the two: these I argue are the themes of epistolary lyric in eighteenth-century France. The unique quality of monophonic epistolary writing depicts these themes clearly, and this quality is none other than Lyric. Lyric writing is always the expression of a desire left unfulfilled within the blankness of white space; epistolary lyric, I argue, presents this expression but also repeats its contrasting silence through blanks in the text. The epistolary writer in the eighteenth century is a poet who seeks presence on the page to make up for an absence in time and space.

Numerous recent publications in the field of eighteenth-century French literary scholarship have opened up new possibilities for readers interested in the female tradition(s). Joan Stewart's *Gynographs* (1993) brought to light French women writers about whom many graduate students had never heard before. In addition, Joan DeJean's *Tender Geographies* (1991) is the cornerstone study for scholars interested in tracing the fate of female authors in the French tradition, and her 1996 volume entitled *Ancients Against Moderns: Culture Wars and the Making of a Fin de Siècle* draws a brilliant analogy between the end of the seventeenth century and the end of our own. DeJean's scholarship prepares the way for innovative considerations of capitulation and resistance on the part of French women writers, such as Katharine Ann Jensen's study entitled *Writing Love: Letters, Women, and the Novel in France, 1605-1776* (1995) and Julia Douthwaite's *Exotic Women* (1996). Elizabeth Cook's *Epistolary Bodies* (1996) elucidates the particularities of an early print culture and its impact on both authors and the reading public. Thomas M. Kavanaugh's *Esthetics of the Moment: Literature and Art in the French Enlightenment* (1996) draws closest to my purposes insofar as it focuses on the esthetics of transience, movement, and the forever-escaping present within the context of visual and literary representation.

All of these volumes contribute significantly to an understanding of eighteenth-century culture and the art and literature that it produced. My hope in the present study is to add to this body of knowledge by describing the poetics of epistolary form within a largely esthetic framework. A perspective that considers the eighteenth century as a period of lyric innovation and evolution rather than disintegration stands to benefit students and scholars interested in the history of poetic form in France. Indeed, scholarly interest in the notion of Enlightenment lyric has already been affirmed by the publication in 1979 of an edited volume entitled *La Poésie en prose des Lumières au Romantisme*. In the introduction to this volume, Jacques Voisine writes convincingly that

> Au cours du siècle des Lumières, ces distinctions marquées, quelles que soient les langues et les littératures européennes, entre la prose et la poésie, tendent à perdre de leur rigueur. L'évolution des genres ... font que de nouveaux rapports s'établissent entre vers et prose, entre prose et poésie, entre poésie et vers. Il s'ensuit que l'on met en question les oppositions jusqu'alors communément admises, de la poésie et de la prose ...

l'idée que la prose peut être poétique semble donc s'affirmer plus ou moins hardiment dans les littératures européennes, entre 1760-1820. (15-16)

Voisine's observations reveal that explorations in literary form were taking place long before the supposed birth of the prose poem with Baudelaire or the mixing of genres advocated by Hugo in his 1827 *Préface de Cromwell*. They further affirm a framework within which to approach the decidedly poetic features of epistolary prose.

My theoretical positioning in this study is influenced by psychoanalytic and feminist discourses, by the unavoidable impact of Deconstruction, and by myth. Although these influences may at first appear to be disparate, it can be argued that they are not so dissimilar. The myths of Demeter-Persephone and Actaeon-Diana that I employ, for example, are stories of desire played out upon bodies and in the space of the gaze. They dramatize the disappearance of presence much in the same way as Lacanian analysis tends to do. The common element in all of these influences is the mediating role of the sign—whether corporal, textual, or visual—within a play of absence and presence. Persephone stands in as an allegorical incarnation for the linguistic sign, the presence of which is nothing more than the marker of an earlier ravishment and an eventual loss of meaning. Feminist inquiry—which refutes the reduction of woman to a being that *lacks*—further informs my critique of a *siècle sans poésie*.[6]

Many individuals have assisted me in my efforts and I am grateful to them all. I would like to express my sincere thanks and gratitude to Carol Sherman, who has been an invaluable teacher and guide. I also thank Fred Clark, UNC Chapel Hill, for encouraging me in the present project.

Grateful acknowledgment is made to the editors of *Romance Quarterly* and *JAISA* (*Journal for the Association for the Interdisciplinary Study of the Arts*) for permission to reprint portions of Chapters Five and Six (respectively) that have previously appeared in those journals. I would also like to acknowledge the valuable

---

[6] Following Elisabeth Bronfen's observation that "[l]ike an aesthetic order, a social order is constituted by virtue of what it seeks to evade," (215) I show how the perceived *lack* of Enlightenment lyric belies a richness of expression masquerading as silence.

institutional support of Agnes Scott College with regard to this project. My colleagues in the Department of Modern Foreign Languages and Literatures at Agnes Scott College have made it a productive place in which to work, and the librarians and students at McCain Library have been very helpful in my efforts to procure research materials. Special thanks are extended to Jackie Klock for her assistance with the proofs. Finally, I thank my family for their devotion and for their constant good cheer.

Prelude:

THE RAVISHMENT OF PERSEPHONE

Commençons donc par écarter tous les faits. In a time that never was, a young maiden named Persephone was out in a flowery meadow on a warm clear day. She was with a group of other young ladies, carefree and unaware of peril. The maidens strode among the grasses picking flowers, their diaphanous gowns billowing in the breeze. Far off on the edge of the meadow, Persephone spied a bloom more exquisite than any she held in her hand. Curious, she drifted away from the others and knelt down to peer into the dark, streaked flower. She stretched out an alabaster hand to grasp its cool, fluttery weight. The next instant she was gone. Later in the dimming light the other maidens placed hands to brow, searching the horizon for her form, but all they could perceive were broken grasses and an untouched bloom.

The myth of the ravishment of Persephone is a narrative pattern of symbols–an allegory–inscribing notions of abandon and death within the drama of human passion. Persephone bent down to pick a flower and the earth split open all around her. Hades surged out of the pit of Night and forced her down. She became the eternal bride of Night, "sitting motionless on her throne for days" (Calasso 219). Persephone's release came through the acts of her mother: Demeter caused every vine to shrivel, every flower to wither, so that the earth upon which mortals dwelled might resemble her own inner landscape of mourning.

Hades released his bride to return to her mother, but not before she ate of a garnet pomegranate with a shadowy skin. That bitter fruit sealed a bargain between the realm of the living and that of the dead: the bargain was negotiated between men (Hermes and

Hades). Persephone rushed into the bright air above, breathing in life yet bearing within her body the seeds of death. Warm in her mother's embrace, she learned that soon she would have to descend to Hell again. Each year her life would be sealed partly in death, and for that sacrifice she would in turn receive life. From that moment on, spring became the sign of Persephone's return.

Persephone's plight lies partly in her knowledge of the unseen, in the grace with which she enacts the burdensome crossing between shadow and light. She has a vision of ruin, yet cannot waste her precious days in the light relating tales of the dark. Roberto Calasso reads the myth of Persephone as a tale signifying a turning point in Greek thought:

> The [Greek] world had reached a point at which the economy of metamorphosis that had sustained it for so long ... was no longer enough. Things had lost their primordial fluidity, had hardened into profile, and the game that had once been played out between one shape and another was now reduced to the mere alternation of appearance and disappearance ... every presence was now enveloped in a far greater cloak of absence. (211-12)

Persephone embodies the notion of alternation between appearance and disappearance that will govern much of my meditation on the nature of lyricism in France in the Age of Enlightenment. Like Orpheus (and unlike Eurydice), she repeatedly crosses the frontier between clarity and obscurity. In the light, she carries within her the memory of fatality. In the Underworld, she muses on that bright unpicked bloom.

Calasso reminds his readers that the flower desired by Persephone (or Kore) was no ordinary flower: "Kore was looking at a narcissus. She was looking at the act of looking ... [s]he was stretching out her hand to pluck that gaze" (209). The flower in this myth can therefore be said to function like a mirror. The mirror offers the promise of knowledge through reflection, even though we know such a promise to be false. So Persephone, more curious than the other maidens, was desirous of knowledge yet was abducted by a violent male God as she stooped to peer. Like the myths of Pandora and Psyche, her story dramatizes a male refusal of the female desire for knowledge. Hades seized the girl to keep as a mirror for his gaze alone.

Before I come forward with my reasons for dwelling on this myth, I would like to consider the polyvalence of the verb "to ravish." Webster provides three meanings for the verb: 1) "to seize and carry away forcibly" 2) "to rape" 3) "to transport with joy or delight." Delight and terror are combined in the word. When we are told that Persephone was ravished, we are to understand either that she was seized forcibly, or that she was raped, or that she was transported with joy or delight. Whose delight? The multiple layers of the word are true to the richness of myth which, like a great poem, calls for any number of possible interpretations and exhausts none. Calasso affirms the ambivalence of the word when he considers that "[s]ome early poets suggest that Persephone felt a 'fatal desire' to be carried off" (209-210).

Lyricism: Desire, Death

My purpose in beginning with the ravishment of Persephone is to construct an allegorical framework within which to approach the question of lyricism in eighteenth-century France. I am employing the figure of Persephone in an allegorical sense in order to present my theory that the lyric voice was "ravished" by a society not able or willing to let it flower. As an allegory for the lyric impulse, Persephone's abduction and re-emergence illustrates the rejection and return of poetry over time. I define the lyric impulse as the personal expression of emotional excess: what Nietzsche calls "the greater excesses in the desire to feel, imagine, and dream new things—consequence of the excesses one has experienced: hunger for excessive feelings" (*Will* 438). As a product of excess, Lyric Art is a sign of surplus; the sign can be made of ink or blue-veined marble or paint. The sign can be static (texts and the plastic arts), kinetic (dance) or immaterial (music). As a sign, Lyric Art signals the "present absence" of that emotion while paradoxically recording its trace. I subscribe to the view of Art as sublimation and believe that the lyric impulse expresses a resurgence of feeling that was previously submerged. The place of this submergence will have to be the unconscious—Hades's shades, Dante's Hell, Conrad's heart of darkness, Beckett's empty stage—the place of the unseen, non-existent image.

Any attempt at defining the lyric inevitably encounters impossibility; as the German Romantic Friedrich Schlegel wrote, it is the very essence of lyric poetry to escape definition: "c'est son essence propre de ne pouvoir qu'éternellement devenir, et jamais s'accomplir" (quoted in Lacoue-Labarthe 112). One no longer speaks of essences or eternal qualities when contemplating literature, though it has become almost commonplace to speak of literature's failure(s). Since Saussure pointed out that difference and arbitrariness govern the relationship of signifier and signified, readers of literature focus on that difference, on the gaps within language, its silence. Still, the "infinite regress" of the divided sign is all we have, so we keep referring to the (absent) thing. It is in this sense that Derrida constructs his outrageous comparison between poetry and a hedgehog–"l'animal jeté sur la route, absolu, solitaire, roulé en boule auprès de soi" (222). Similarly, W.R. Johnson resorts to the image of a peacock to describe the "changing permanence" of the lyric mode:

> I regard this genre [Lyric] as immutable and universal. Its accidents may and always do show extraordinary variations as it unfolds in time, but its substance abides. As an emblem of this changing permanence, I take Tertullian's brief meditation on the peacock:
>
>> multicolor et discolor et versicolor, numquam ipsa, semper alia, et si semper ipsa quando alia, totiens denique mutanda quotiens movenda. (2)

Johnson's thesis on the resilience of the lyric impulse informs my view that during the Age of Enlightenment lyricism was dormant but not absent.

Where Johnson's peacock-emblem signifies changing permanence, my goddess-emblem signifies mediation and recuperation. I read Persephone's periodic descent into and resurgence from the Underworld as an allegory for the various concentrations and evasions of lyric poetry in the French tradition over time. In this theoretical context, Persephone's return corresponds to a reappearance of the lyric impulse made possible by a revaluation on the part of society. Persephone's descent consequently corresponds to a comparative "winter" of lyricism in the French tradition. My purpose in making of Persephone an allegory of Lyricism is to refute the notion of a *crise de poésie* in eighteenth-century France by delineating a theory of epistolary lyric.

As an allegorical figure of the Lyric, Persephone offers above all the ideal of a dual participation that defies both division and opposition. That is to say that she resides equally in the domains of the seen and the unseen. More specifically, she may be seen as the embodiment of movement between the two realms, signifying her own absence corporally each time she reappears. Likewise, lyric poetry reveals more than it says, and suggests its own absence through the blank margins of the page. As an allegorical figure of the Lyric, Persephone weaves a veil between known and unknown, above and below, *l'extérieur* and *l'intérieur*. Now it is not arbitrary that such an allegorical figure is feminine, for the female body is the physical locus of transformation from nonbeing to being. As a point of origin, "Woman" connotes the uncanny emblem of passage from nonbeing to life and back again. Elisabeth Bronfen summarizes Western attitudes toward the female body by calling it "the site of conjunction between more than one order, that which is in excess of an order, an impossibility within the system, a vanishing point or oscillation between absence and presence" (214-15).

Persephone-as-Lyric allows us to consider the lyric as a point of passage between language as communication and language as abstraction. The Lyric is the point in Art at which the reader or viewer sees the creator looking within. When T.S. Eliot writes in "The Waste Land"

> I could not
> Speak, and my eyes failed, I was neither
> Living nor dead, and I knew nothing,
> Looking into the heart of light, the silence. (64)

one senses that he has looked within and that his poem on the page is the expression of that moment of excess.

Nietzsche aligns the idea of excess with the Dionysiac spirit, which he defines through opposition to the Apollonian spirit:

> Apollo, as an ethical deity, demands moderation from his followers and, in order to maintain it, self-knowledge. And thus the admonitions 'Know thyself' and 'Nothing to excess!' coexist with the aesthetic necessity of beauty, while hubris and excess are considered the truly hostile spirits of the non-Apolline realm....
> (*Birth* 26)

It is not difficult to see that poetry lies on the other side of moderation and therefore opposes the Apollonian ideal.

Lyric poetry is associated with Dionysian notions of disorder and desire because it crosses over the boundary between thee and me. The lyric poet tells the reader "Know thyself by knowing me." Here again the idea of the threshold or passage is prevalent; the myth of Persephone reveals her to be an intermediary between two separated realms. These opposed realms have been assigned several terms by several brilliant minds: Nietzsche opposes Apollo and Dionysus, Freud casts into conflict ego and id, and Lacan differentiates between the Symbolic and the Imaginary. Julia Kristeva, perhaps most convincingly, names the semiotic as an erratic force that defines poetic language through the fact that it lies outside the accepted system of linguistic signifiers (Marks/de Courtivon 165). I take the lyric in literature to be the expression of this force, expressing mediation between our primary and secondary processes.[1]

ROSES

Roberto Calasso tells us that in abducting Persephone

> Hades was claiming the supremacy of a world that was *other*: isolated, separate, and silent. But this other world culminated in the flower of the visible, and that flower was Persephone. (208)

I would like to add to the allegorical figure of Persephone-as-Lyric the layer of this flower. In other words, I am taking this flower to be a concrete emblem of the lyric impulse and have picked the rose to be the genus of flower. Neither Persephone (coded in death) nor flower (coded always in femininity) can fully stand in for the lyric, precisely because the maiden never picked the flower. Had she picked the narcissus whose deep-hued light caused her to stray, things might have happened differently. Contemplation and self-possession might have overcome aggression as the means to self-knowl-

---

[1] Writing on Charles Rycroft, A.S. Byatt explains that according to this psychoanalyst primary process "works with symbols, hallucinations and verbal images, following no rules of logic, space or time" while secondary process is "conscious thought governed by reason, respect for grammar and logic" (261).

edge. Hades abducts Persephone in order to have a bride at his side, an outside identity through which to know himself. Indeed, the act of ravishing the maiden is nothing more than the gesture of self-assertion through possession of another: this is the same gesture performed by Valmont in Laclos's *Les Liaisons dangereuses*, by Lovelace in Richardson's *Clarissa*, and by the third Mother-Superior in Diderot's *La Religieuse*. It is an empty gesture that always fails, a vain claim to selfhood through domination of another.

As a concrete emblem of lyricism, the rose that blooms "all by itself" can be likened to poetic tropes that ignore the grammatical economy. Entirely self-contained, the rose is a sign of desire and death as well as the preeminent emblem of femininity. These connotations—beauty, purity, transience, death—code the rose as an emblem of lyricism. I consider the lyric tradition in France as a single rose "that closes and opens" (cummings 35) across centuries of time. Like Persephone, whose reappearance marks a rebirth of life even as it signals its eventual cessation, this opening and closing reveals an alternating movement that is at the heart of lyricism.

The first full bloom of lyricism is *Le Roman de la rose*. In Guillaume de Lorris's portion of the romance, *celui qui dit je* is a dreamer, a poet, and a courtly lover. Having penetrated the inner bower of the garden he comes across the fountain of Narcissus, inside of which he spies an irresistible rose bud:

> Entre ces boutons en eslui
> Un si tres bel, qu'envers celui
> Nus des autres riens ne prisé
> Puisque je l'oi bien avisé;
> Car une color l'enlumine
> Qui est si vermeille et si fine
> Con Nature la pot plus faire ...
> Ains m'en apressai por lui prendre,
> Si g'i osasse la main tendre ...
> Espines tranchans et aguës,
> Orties et ronces crochues
> Ne me lessierent avant traire,
> Que je m'en cremoie mal faire.
> (82-83, lines 1655-61, 1673-74, 1677-80)

Echoing the myth of Persephone, the narrator draws in close to the promise of self-reflection and self-knowledge only to be thwarted when he attempts possession of the promise. At the exact moment when he stretches out his hand Amors drives the shaft of an arrow through his eye, causing him to faint as he realizes "li cuers me ment" (83, line 1701). As in the Greek myth, desire for possession is born in the illusory space of the gaze and is destroyed in the concrete act of touch. The destruction of the illusion results in a symbolic death: this narrator's swoon, Persephone's abduction, Mistress Henley's ambiguous final words.

Guillaume de Lorris's 4,058-line allegory of the rose inaugurated the lyric tradition in France. The next full bloom of lyricism occurred with Ronsard, whose "rose poems" occupy a central place in the canon of French literature. With Ronsard the rose—and therefore the lyric poem—becomes less an abstraction and more a concrete emblem of transience:

> La grâce dans sa feuille et l'amour se repose,
> Embaumant les jardins et les arbres d'odeur;
> Mais, battue ou de pluie ou d'excessive ardeur,
> Languissante elle meurt, feuille à feuille déclose.
> ("Les Amours de Marie," quoted in Allem, 285)

> Las! voyez comme en peu d'espace,
> Mignonne, elle a dessus la place,
> Las! las! ses beautés laissé choir!
> O vraiment marâtre Nature,
> Puis qu'une telle fleur ne dure
> Que du matin jusques au soir!
> ("Ode à Cassandre," quoted in Allem, 289)

Ronsard's rose is a bloom so far open it is falling apart: Guillaume de Lorris's untouched bud has opened into the full flower of death. With Ronsard, the lyric voice weds Eros and Thanatos. Their volatile union—which is nothing less than the dark union of Hades and Persephone—is the excess that creates images and tropes in language.

Ronsard's baroque rose is spun of night, of death's repose. After Ronsard, the rose—still my metaphor for the lyric tradition—hardens into classical form. It is as if the silk bud of medieval lyricism and the velvet fallen petal of Renaissance lyricism become, in seventeenth-century France, a breakable painted rose. As if made of glass, the lyric poem in Classical France is no longer an organic *objet langagier* but rather an artificial *objet décoratif*. The neoclassical poet (defined primarily by Boileau in his *Art poétique*) should strive to express him or herself in clear, precise rhetoric. Under the influence of Boileau, the rose emblematizes neither an intimate dream of desire (Lorris) nor a personal metaphor of loss (Ronsard); instead, it is an impersonal object. The influence of classical taste upon the lyric tradition can be demonstrated in Malherbe's "Consolation à Monsieur du Perier sur la mort de sa fille":

> Mais elle estoit du monde, où les plus belles choses
>   Ont le pire destin,
> Et rose, elle a vescu ce que vivent les roses,
>   L'espace d'un matin.
>
> (Martinon 101)

These lines illustrate the *cool refusal* of lyric poetry that accompanied the influence of Descartes and *le Siècle des Lumières*: poetry itself becomes one of the "plus belles choses [qui] ont le pire destin." With Malherbe the lyric poem is stripped of the intimate *je qui parle* and is infiltrated by a dry third-person discourse of reason. The admonishment to Reason that the poet extends to his friend –"Est-ce quelque dedale où ta raison perduë/Ne se retreuve pas?"–is cold comfort indeed.

Before I begin to focus exclusively on the question of Enlightenment poetics I would like to pursue this rose of lyricism, continuing with Condillac and ending with Mallarmé.[2] By the time of Condillac's *Traité des sensations*–1749–a shift had gradually been taking place in the perceptions and in the minds of the thinkers of that age. Indeed, physical perception had begun to supersede the notion of innate ideation as the source of human cognition. With the death of Louis XIV in 1715 the political notion of *pouvoir absolu* became increasingly undermined; Pleasure reigned. In a philosophical context, the Cartesian philosophy of *innéisme* found an adversary in the *sensualisme* of Locke and Condillac.

Locke saw the mind as pure white paper–"void of all characters"–and asserted that "all ideas come from sensation or reflec-

---

[2] I do not undertake a discussion of lyric poetry after Mallarmé in this context, for the complexities of twentieth-century poetic form are beyond the scope of this study. A.S. Byatt identifies Mallarmé's "language flowers" as mental icons after which there have been only "ghosts of ghosts of roses" (12).

tion" (77). Drawing upon Locke, Condillac linked sensation with the acquisition of knowledge, holding forth the example of a statue whose very being is blended with the odor of rose:

> Si nous lui présentons une rose, elle sera par rapport à nous une statue qui sent une rose; mais par rapport à elle, elle ne sera que l'odeur même de cette fleur.
> Elle sera donc odeur de rose, d'oeillet, de jasmin, de violette, suivant les objets qui agiront sur son organe. En un mot, les odeurs ne sont à cet égard que ses propres modifications ou manières d'être.... (41)

Beyond the obvious importance of this blending of physical sensation and philosophy—*je sens donc je suis*—I find Condillac's enumeration of different flowers intriguing. His seemingly gratuitous naming of other genuses of flower—carnation, jasmine, violet—serves to illustrate Locke's second source of rational thought, which is reflection. In transposing his garland of thought onto paper, Condillac's "thinking rose" replaces the ornamentation of Classical taste with a new emphasis on cognition.

By the time of Mallarmé, the rose as both object and metaphor disappears willfully and necessarily. What began as a pristine bud in Lorris's medieval romance and, dying, opened slowly across time now vanishes into the recesses of a new ideal—the ideal of suggestion and pure abstraction:

> *Nommer* un objet, c'est supprimer les trois quarts de la jouissance du poème qui est faite du bonheur de deviner peu à peu; le *suggérer*, voilà le rêve.... ("Sur l'évolution littéraire" 392)

> Je dis: une fleur! et, hors de l'oubli où ma voix relègue aucun contour, en tant que quelque chose d'autre que les calices sus, musicalement se lève, idée même et suave, l'absente de tous bouquets. ("Crise de vers" 251)

With Mallarmé, the lyric poet can merely suggest forms, not represent them. The poem is an evocation created by blank space and by constellations of words; the price of this pure lyricism is nothing less than the poet's own "disparition élocutoire" ("Crise de vers" 248).

Mallarmé's ideas caused a revolution in the poetic language of his contemporaries and his successors, yet are Mallarmean notions not already present with the Greeks? Plato's allegory of the cave presents just such a relation between shadow and form, between Idea and thing. And what ultimate difference can be ascertained between Mallarmé's flower–*l'absente de tous bouquets*–and the narcissus that Persephone never picked? At the instant of her abduction Persephone dropped her bouquet in fright, and that bouquet was incomplete. Mallarmé expressed the absence of the referent; but he did not invent it, for there was nothing to invent. Mallarmean absence recapitulates the expression of lack; in so doing, it formulates the paradox of all lyric expression, which is to mark a loss of presence.

If I have insisted in pursuing these roses as warm blushes of lyricism in France, it is in order to establish a framework within which to approach the question of lyricism in the French Enlightenment. Gathering the "roses" of Guillaume de Lorris, Ronsard, Malherbe, Condillac, and Mallarmé into a kind of literary garland over time, I have suggested that the lyric tradition thrived over time. The rose, moreover, stands in as a sign of Persephone, herself an allegory of Lyricism's *errance*. The rose and the mythical goddess are emblems through which I am attempting to apprehend and express the nature of lyricism. They stand in intimate relation to femininity, desire, death, and the gaze–all crucial aspects of the lyric poem. More important, however, is the alternating movement inscribed by Persephone and suggested by the rose. Persephone alternates between fatal stasis in the Underworld and the periodic rush to warm life above. The rose, too, opens and closes, flowering fully from the pen of Ronsard, or retreating under the cold eye of Malherbe.

e.e. cummings writes in one of his love poems

> (i do not know what it is about you that closes
> and opens; only something in me understands
> the voice of your eyes is deeper than all roses) (44)

Linking gaze and rose just as Guillaume de Lorris did seven centuries earlier, cummings captures something of the necessarily unknowable nature of lyricism by lauding the opening and closing of his *bien-aimée*. I submit that Persephone's crossing from Underworld to Earth dramatizes the concept of poetic mediation between the poet's unconscious and his or her conscious life. The mournful maiden who traverses death's frontier and the rose "rendering death and forever with each breathing" (cummings 44) both perform the primary movement of the lyric voice, which is an alternating veiling and unveiling of sense and its absence, darkness and light.

SIÈCLE DES LUMIÈRES, SIÈCLE SANS POÈTES?

If I have demonstrated something of the nature of the lyric impulse in the French tradition, it is in the hopes of approaching the nature of Lyric in the post-classical age. The Enlightenment in France is generally understood to be a time in which the Classical doctrine continued to enjoy favor; the very term *Lumières* reflects such an esthetic preference. The definition of classical taste that Nietzsche provides in *The Will to Power in Art* provides insight into current inherited notions of the term:

> To grasp that a quantum of coldness, lucidity, hardness is part of all 'classical' taste: logic above all, happiness in spirituality, 'three unities,' concentration, hatred for feeling, heart, *esprit*, hatred of the manifold, uncertain, rambling, for intimations ... logical-psychological simplification. Contempt for detail, complexity, the uncertain. (447-48)

The excellence of Nietzsche's definition lies in its alternation between telling what classical taste is and what it is not. E.B.O. Borgerhoff affirms this kind of definition by exclusion when he writes of a fundamental "desire for aesthetic purity" in the context of French Classicism (243). According to Borgerhoff, it is this desire for purity of form that precluded the possibility of the mixing of generic categories. The seventeenth century, he explains, existed "in tension, as a paradox ... of the form-creating and form-destroying capacity of human spirituality" (244).

The ideal of *pure form* influenced French thought well into the eighteenth century and even reached into the nineteenth century with the poetry of *Le Parnasse*. Yet as an ideal, the apprehension of pure form was impossible. Although Racine perhaps attained it, it was not enough. It was too perfect. In the postclassical era, therefore, the notion of pure form became the obstacle that made possible a passage to *transparence*.³ Now transparency here does not mean the impersonal taste of Classicism but rather the post-classical transparency of the unseen: not reflection but refraction, the knowledge of something hidden—*la transparence infranchissable*. It is not a plain ray of light but rather one passing through *un obstacle léger*: an eye, a veil, a printed page. It is light diffused through passage: the passage of time between the absolute power of a King and that of a Regent, the passing of winter that brings Persephone's return. It is Marivaux's Sylvia, still masked, saying softly to herself "Ah! je vois clair dans mon coeur" (*Jeu* Act II, scene xii, 87).

Still masked, and alone: is this not the very situation of lyric poetry in post-classical France? Is it possible that disguise and isolation allowed the lyric poet to overcome an esthetic hostile to his or her power? Because of her mask, Sylvia sees "clear in her heart": pretending to be someone else shows her who she is and whom she loves. Now this principle set forth by the poet Marivaux in *Le Jeu de l'amour et du hasard* exemplifies both the post-classical notion of *transparence* and the dilemma of the poet in Enlightenment France. Transparency is revealed in the declaration *je vois clair dans mon coeur*: my heart is the last place I can clearly see, and yet it is the impossibility of the symbolic act that prompts me to try.

The Enlightenment took pains to preserve what it purported to refuse, namely the poetic, the personal, the lyric voice. Like the Apollonian consciousness that hid, "like a veil," Dionysian forces from view (Nietzsche *Birth* 21), the collective mind of the Enlightenment pushed lyricism down in the name of clarity and Reason. E.B.O. Borgerhoff describes the problematic nature of this rationalist gesture of suppression when he writes that

> there appears to be another sort of classicism, more characteristic of the Eighteenth Century, which is indeed reasonable and which is for the moment contented because it seems to have resolved the paradox. But it is an imitative and lifeless classicism because with its idealism it solved, or thought it solved, only the intellectual problem, and this solution was possible ... only by denying ... the artistic problem. (244)

---

³ Here I am indebted to Jean Starobinski's book *Jean-Jacques Rousseau: La Transparence et l'obstacle*.

Indeed, the "artistic problem"–affect vs. intellect, or in Georges May's terms, *réalisme/moralisme*–played itself out in the relatively freer form of epistolary prose. Epistolary writing allowed for an easing of tensions between philosophical, epistemological, and emotional discourses. In avowing itself as being far from the ideal, it created a space for the post-classical writer to negotiate the "fall" from pure form.

What I aim to demonstrate through a study of epistolary texts is that the act of pushing down betrays a passion: "[l]ike an aesthetic order, a social order is constituted by virtue of what it seeks to evade" (Bronfen 215). In the following chapters I shall demonstrate that epistolary writing contains all of the elements at odds with the esthetic doctrine of Classicism: the polymorphous, the uncertain, the erratic, complexity, uncertainty (Nietzsche *Will* 50). Behind a decorous mask of circumstance (the letter as *trouvaille*), moral purpose ("J'ai vu les moeurs de mon temps, et j'ai publié ces lettres"), or anonymity (the mask of many *épistolières*), *le moi s'exprime*. I shall return at greater length to the formal structures of epistolary lyric in Part One. Now I would like to examine the notion of letter (and of literature generally) as mask and to take into account the contrast I am constructing between epistolary lyric and the actual verse poetry of eighteenth-century France.

In a paragraph that begins with the unsettling equation "Le roman est une mort," Roland Barthes makes the flamboyant claim that

> Le passé simple et la troisième personne du Roman, ne sont rien d'autre que ce geste fatal par lequel l'écrivain montre du doigt le masque qu'il porte. Toute la Littérature peut dire: *Larvatus prodeo*, je m'avance en désignant mon masque du doigt.
> (*Degré* 37)

Barthes does not decipher his statement, preferring to leave his readers puzzling over it. The first way to tap into this passage is to remember that the epistolary novel is a genre distinguished not by the third person but by the first; the presence of the *je qui parle* draws epistolary writing away from the mimetic tradition of *vraisemblance* and nearer to the lyrical tradition. Next, the declaration *Larvatus prodeo* must be considered since, as Barthes tells us, it is the motto of Descartes. Perhaps readers would have done well to ponder this curve-ball hurled by Descartes. Could it be that the philosopher himself appreciated and played with the meaning of his own *je pense donc je suis*?

As for Barthes's statement that all literature acts as a mask, the notion is intriguing even if its accuracy is both immeasurable and irrelevant. What is true is that writing (like painting) is a covering over of blank surface: *ut pictura poesis*. If we compare this act of covering to the act of sculpting we see that the latter is one of extraction. Each act obeys a different god, and each act alludes to the other. Writing and painting mask–cover over–a purity and an absence where sculpting *presents* these same ideas in three dimensions. The statue, Roberto Calasso explains, is the "[m]essenger of the realm of appearance" (246) and the epitome of Greek elegance, which "arises from excavation, from the cavity" (240). It is a creation formed by removal and "carved out of the air" (Calasso 240). Classical taste finds the statue pleasing, whereas literature and visual art (including theater) are troubling since they create meaning through acts of concealment. Poetry, moreover, was perhaps the worst culprit since it imitates statuesque contours on the page even as it covers pure white space. The uncanny ability of the poem to mask or cover the page while at the same time leaving it blank is perhaps the source of the uneasiness poetry inspires. From Plato to the eighteenth-century philosophers and to this day, poetry is an art met with anxiety and suspicion.

LE BEAU ET LE VRAI

What did these philosophers actually say about the poetry of their day? It is necessary to delineate the tenor of this suspicion before turning to epistolary lyricism and returning to Persephone. While it is untrue that the eighteenth century in France was literally a *siècle sans poètes*[4] it is generally accepted that notions of "absolute literary authority"–as outlined by Boileau in the seventeenth century–

---

[4] Among the eighteenth-century Francophone poets who wrote in verse are Voltaire, Jean-Baptiste Rousseau, Jean-Jacques Le Franc de Pompignan, Jacques Delille, Ecouchard Lebrun, and André Chénier. The Dutch-born writer Isabelle de Charrière also wrote verse poetry in the manner of the seventeenth-century *précieuses*.

continued to influence writers greatly (DeJean *TG* 164). The *authority* of actual verse poetry, or that which seemingly created its esthetic value, was still predicated upon the use of the *alexendrin* and on codified rules for versification and rhetoric.

In the period that followed the death of Louis XIV, the supposed refusal of the lyric voice in the early part of the century emerged as the legacy of Malherbe and Boileau. Malherbe pruned the French language of ornament, Italianate taste, and metaphor, finding all of these to be both decadent and excessive. Similarly, Boileau's motto in his *Art poétique* serves as a summation of the neoclassical view of poetry: "rien n'est beau que le vrai, le vrai seul est aimable." Joan DeJean reminds her readers that Boileau's influence upon the French tradition and canon formation cannot be underestimated, writing that "[t]he founding moment of canon formation in France begins in the late seventeenth century and continues until the middle of the eighteenth century" (*TG* 183). Thus the early Enlightenment, DeJean affirms, was still very much under the influence of Boileau's authority.

For early Enlightenment thinkers, truth and Beauty were not equated, as they were to become in the mind of Keats: rather, truth alone is beautiful (Boileau) and beauty is never truthful. Voltaire in particular spans the passage from the Neoclassical period into the early modern period, and one notices in his works a kind of equivocal adherence to the classical esthetic that belies an anxiety of influence. Voltaire remains particularly suspicious of poetry; he writes for example in *Les Lois de Minos*

> que les vers soient harmonieux et bien faits; mérite absolument nécessaire, sans lequel la poésie n'est jamais qu'un monstre....
> (171)

Here Voltaire considers that without order, poetic language would become a *monster*. In his 1778 work *Irène* he repeats the warning about the potential monstrosity of poetic language, saying that Racine demonstrated inimitable genius in verse and that the finest prose works are merely attempts to equal the art of Racine:

> les vers sont une langue qu'il est donné à très peu d'esprits de posséder ... [m]ais les ouvrages de prose dans lesquels on a mieux imité le style de Racine sont ce que nous avons de

meilleur dans notre langue. Point de vrai succès aujourd'hui sans cette correction, sans cette pureté qui seule met le génie dans tout son jour, et sans laquelle ce génie ne déploierait qu'une force *monstrueuse*, tombant à chaque pas dans une faiblesse plus *monstrueuse*.... (329, my emphasis)

For Voltaire, language that lacks the classical expression of precision and purity may become monstrous, which is to say denatured, uncivilized, and base. The anxiety of influence mentioned above has to do with Voltaire's allegience to Racine as the perfect model, for how, he asks, can any poet improve upon Racine? After Racine exhausted the capacities of verse, he implies, writers began to resort to prose.

Indeed, in his own oeuvre Voltaire best expresses the new preoccupations of his age in prose. While his dramatic verse reflects some innovations, such as the treatment of religious themes and a greater attention to costume and décor (Clouard 316), it is in prose that Voltaire is able to go beyond the influence of masters such as Racine in order to express theological concepts (in *Candide*) as well as philosophical views *(Zadig, Micromégas)*. While he warned against what he called the monstrous possibilities of unfettered expression, Voltaire concedes that for him, verse poetry had reached its apex in the theater of Racine. Although he continued to praise the codified rules of versification and to rely upon the *alexendrin* in his own dramatic writing, he ceded a new authority to prose.

Dramatic Lyricism and Epistolary Lyricism

If we consider lyric poetry to be one of *les plus belles choses du monde*, it follows as Malherbe tells us that it will inevitably encounter *le pire destin*. The worst possible destiny for poetry is to be ignored (unread) or scorned. By the end of the seventeenth century verse poetry had become an object of ridicule, suffering the latter fate. Affectation and preciosity had infiltrated the genre to the extent that the poet was considered to be a fop and a fake, as seen in Molière's caricature:

ORONTE: Mais ne puis-je savoir ce que dans mon sonnet ...

ALCESTE: Franchement, il est bon à mettre au cabinet;
Vous vous êtes réglé sur de méchants modèles,
Et vos expressions ne sont point naturelles [...]

> Ce n'est que jeu de mots, qu'affectation pure,
> Et ce n'est point ainsi que parle la nature.
> Le méchant goût du siècle en cela me fait peur;
> Nos pères, tout grossiers, l'avaient beaucoup meilleur [....]
> *(Le Misanthrope* I,ii p. 45)

Already in the seventeenth century, pure lyricism had taken refuge in another genre–tragic theater. For it is only Racine who can be counted among the great lyric poets of *le Grand Siècle*, who expressed his voice through the ready-made shadow-masks of ancient Greek myth. Behind Phèdre, Hippolyte, and Thésée there is always and only Racine, upon whom the veil of genius heavily weighed.

W.R. Johnson offers a meditation on the migratory nature of lyric that I quote at length, since it illustrates the link between dramatic lyricism in seventeenth-century France and epistolary lyricism in the French Enlightenment:

> As lyric is the most elusive of generic forms, so is it the most protean, the most unstable of generic impulses. When the lyric poet casts his poem in the first-person singular (personal or fictive), in lyric meter, the integrity of lyric form and lyric impulse remains intact. But when the lyric poet undertakes to write drama, he does not necessarily become a dramatist, nor, when he undertakes to write a novel, does he necessarily become a novelist. What tends to happen in either case is that drama and novel become lyricized: the invaded genre endures some degree of mutation when lyric purposes usurp its form and ignore its customary objects of mimesis; and the lyric impulse itself, either diminished or uncannily nourished by its imposture, is also transformed. (149)

Johnson's thesis supports my interpretation of the "ravishment" of lyricism by the Classical doctrine, by Reason, and by the early *philosophes*. Like Persephone, who was wedded to Night but then returned to Light, the lyric voice was silenced and then learned to sing anew. Still, the important point is that upon its return the lyric voice is changed utterly. Johnson affirms that the "invaded genre" is transformed by lyric purposes and vice versa.

The lyric impulse in France was "ravished" during the reign of the Sun-King and did not "return" in pure form–verse poems written in the first-person singular—until the nineteenth century. During that time, it remade itself in different forms: Persephone wandering over earth with dark poppies in her hair. First it transformed itself into dramatic lyric with Racine. Next it transformed itself into epistolary lyric with Rousseau.

W.R. Johnson's innovative thesis on the changing permanence of lyric fails to take into account the epistolary novel. He writes that

> [t]he novel is less prone to such [lyrical] possession than the drama probably because, since its natural mode is the anonymous, distanced narrator, it offers considerable resistance to lyric intrusions and temperings ... narrative tends to be fairly secure against lyrical aggression. (149)

Epistolary texts do not conform to this definition of the novel since they necessarily employ first-person singular narration. Epistolary (non)-narrative is not at all "secure" against lyrical "aggression" (I prefer to think of the lyrical presence in prose not as an aggression but as a happy union). The letter-text offered no resistance whatsoever to "lyrical intrusions," nor did the writer who adopted the lyrical letter as her preferred mode of discourse. On the contrary, the epistolary narrator cultivates the personal expression of emotion.

Critics generally agree that in the Age of Enlightenment the shadow-discourse of lyricism took refuge in prose:

> On a accoutumé de juger le XVIIIe siècle comme un *siècle sans poésie*. Qu'est-ce à dire? La poésie peut-elle disparaître momentanément du monde ... [n]'est-ce pas plutôt l'idée que nous nous faisons de la poésie qui se révèle insuffisante, puisqu'elle est incapable de rendre compte de ce qui s'écrivit au cours de ce siècle? Il serait bon de revenir à une notion plus large de la poésie ... [o]ù s'était réfugiée la poésie ...? On la retrouve, masquée et timide, comme craintive d'elle-même, dans la prose.... (Roudat 9, 21 my emphasis)

In the following chapters I shall examine this displacement of lyric purpose to narrative form. I shall demonstrate how the epistolary text becomes transformed by the poetic influx of blank space, rhetorical tropes, and first-person singular narration. I shall propose that a fifty-page text inscribing nothing beyond a *je* calling out for an absent *tu* should no longer be called a novel. Concentrating on texts authored by women, I shall credit epistolary lyricism for bridging the doctrine of Classicism with the awakening of Romanticism. Finally, I shall laud the *épistolière* for nurturing the lyric impulse and willing it to survive in letters. Through Demeter's recuperative gesture Persephone is reborn.

Zilia

I began this Prelude with a retelling of a mythical abduction; I would like to conclude by considering Zilia's capture as an echo of that myth. Following her "Introduction historique" in which she idealizes Peruvian culture and relates the Spanish conquest of Peru, Madame de Graffigny begins her epistolary text *in medias res* by having Zilia recount her abduction by Spanish captors to her absent lover Aza:

> Depuis le moment terrible (qui aurait dû être arraché de la chaîne du temps, et replongé dans les idées éternelles) depuis le moment d'horreur où ces sauvages impies m'ont enlevée au culte du Soleil, à moi-même, à ton amour ... je n'éprouve que les effets du malheur.... (Letter 1, 257)

Here in her first letter Zilia describes her abduction above all as a separation from herself: "ces sauvages impies m'ont enlevée ... à moi-même." Immediately, Graffigny's protagonist juxtaposes light and darkness metaphorically in order to express the violence inflicted upon her by her "ravishers," whom she names as such:

> Plongée dans un abîme d'obscurité, mes jours sont semblables aux nuits les plus effrayantes.
> Loin d'être touchés de mes plaintes, mes ravisseurs ne le sont pas même de mes larmes; sourds à mon langage, ils n'entendent pas mieux les cris de mon desespoir. (Letter 1, 257)

The darkness into which the Peruvian princess is thrust echoes the Underworld that engulfed Persephone as she stooped to pick a flower. Here the image of the obscure abyss serves to introduce the theme of incommunicability, which remains primary throughout the text. Already in this passage Zilia laments her inability to make her thoughts known; her male captors are "deaf" both to her verbal pleas and her non-verbal signs of distress (tears, cries). Linguistically isolated and physically violated, Zilia writes of traversing a seemingly fatal passage:

> Le temps s'écoule, les ténèbres succèdent à la lumière ... du suprême bonheur, je suis tombée dans l'horreur du désespoir, sans qu'aucun intervalle m'ait préparée à cet affreux passage. (Letter 1, 258)

The symbolic passage is described by Zilia as a downward fall into despair and as an "awful passage." Her description codes her violation as a kind of death. Her passage is an irrevocable fall from a state of innocence and wholeness to a state of division from self.

While the experience of violation itself is irreversible, its expression is not. Like Persephone who conquers the shadow by becoming its messenger, Zilia survives by telling the transgression she has endured. Her language, importantly, is neither verbal nor corporal; rather it is as Graffigny explains in a footnote "un grand nombre de petits cordons de différentes couleurs" (Letter 1, 258). Zilia's "verses" are knots turned and twisted in colored cord–the image calls to mind W.R. Johnson's lyrical "versicolored" peacock. Zilia's "quipos" begs the question of *écriture féminine*; this is a question that has been skillfully addressed by Nancy K. Miller (*Subject to Change*) and by Katherine Ann Jensen (*Writing Love*).

In the myth of Persephone and in Graffigny's novel, an initial violation (the ravishment) can be identified ultimately as the origin of creation (Spring in the myth, the letters themselves in Graffigny's text). A symbolic death becomes a harbinger of renewed life: "pendant la nuit, je courus à mes *quipos*, et profitant du silence ... je me hâtai de les nouer, dans l'espérance qu'avec leur secours je rendrais immortelle l'histoire de notre amour" (Graffigny 258). *Pendant la nuit*: night is necessary to the flowering of voice, as is silence. Both allow for the "terrible moment" of experience to be transformed into the "eternal ideas" of expression through Art (Graffigny 257).

The word ravishment, in all its ambiguity, captures the complex rapports between masculinity and femininity, possession and submission. I have adopted the myth of Persephone's ravishment in order to frame my inquiry into the nature of lyricism during the French Enlightenment. During this era, I have suggested, lyric poetry was "ravished" by a discourse of Reason and by an emphasis on epistemological and scientific progress. Curiously, however, the *ravishment* of sentiment and personality ultimately served to preserve the lyric voice. Staging the drama of its own mortal passage, the lyric impulse went underground in letters, masking itself in epistolary form.

PART I: STRUCTURES IN EPISTOLARY LYRIC

I

L'ECHANGE UNILATÉRAL: SOLITUDE

The primary texts with which I am concerned in the present inquiry are all epistolary "novels" written by women in the middle and late eighteenth century: Madame de Graffigny's *Lettres d'une Péruvienne* (1747), Madame Riccoboni's *Lettres de Mistress Fanni Butlerd* (1757) and *Lettres de Milady Juliette Catesby à Milady Henriette Campley, son amie* (1759), and Madame de Charrière's *Lettres de Mistress Henley* (1784). All represent monophonic epistolary narratives and illustrate the nature of epistolary lyric. The scholarship of Jean Rousset and Janet Altman has been instrumental in leading me to shape my own research, and I shall make frequent reference to their work here.

Rousset separates all epistolary texts into two categories: those that feature "la voix soliste" and those that employ "[de] grandes organisations symphoniques" (FS 76). An example of the first would be *Lettres portugaises*; an example of the second, *Les Liaisons dangereuses*: this division can also be described by the contrasting terms *monophonic* and *polyphonic*. He then identifies two subcategories within the monophonic register. First there is "la suite à une voix: une seule personne écrit, le plus souvent à un seul destinataire" (76); he cites *Lettres portugaises* and *Lettres d'une Péruvienne* (although Zilia technically has two *destinataires*). Second there is

> la variante de l'échange unilatéral ... une seule personne écrit, [pourtant] le destinataire est atteint, les contacts sont établis, invisibles pour le lecteur, mais cependant perceptibles; les réponses ne sont pas reproduites, mais il y a des réponses. (Rousset FS 78)

He calls this variant "un duo dont on n'entend qu'une voix" (78) and lists as an example Mme Riccoboni's *Lettres de Mistress Fanni Butlerd.*

In the context of lyricism, the monophonic epistolary text comes closest to the border between novel and poem; indeed the letter may be read as a kind of hybrid among journal entry, poem, and dramatic monologue. Like the lyric poet, the letter-writer is alone but is conscious of a reader and writes accordingly. In this sense she resembles somewhat the *personnage de théâtre* delivering a monologue: she speaks to herself although she knows that what she says (writes) will be heard (read). Unlike both the poet and theatrical character, however, the solitary letter-writer expects—or at least hopes for—a response. As Rousset has demonstrated by devising his variant of the unilateral exchange, that response seldom comes: this he calls *la suite à une voix.* The page is a stage upon which a woman appears and speaks, though the auditorium is empty. Paradoxically it is the lack of response that allows for the woman's richness of speech.

Form, Rousset insists, dictates meaning. A letter conveys meaning in ways that both dramatic dialogue and non-epistolary prose do not. In its case, the dynamic of sender and receiver and the letter as simulacrum or "pseudopresence" (Altman 140) code language in specific, poetic ways. This chapter and the two that follow delineate a poetics of the epistolary code. In general terms, this code has been characterized as "the language of absence" (Altman 140) and as a discourse "[qui] se cherche et se constitue" (Rousset FS 65). With its unremitting emphasis on separation in space and time, the letter confirms the solitude of both writer and reader. In addition, fictional letters emphasize abstraction over narration by privileging rhetorical ambiguity and by destabilizing the notion of language as a linguistic economy.

Monophonic epistolary writing destabilizes the notion of communication. The very term *unilateral exchange* captures the central paradox of epistolary writing: I am separated from you in time and/or space, yet by writing a letter I enter into an ersatz exchange. The letter is *une voie à sens unique:* here I mean both that the letter physically travels a one-way street (moving from point A to point B) and that its meaning is univocal. Its "unique meaning" can always be reduced to the simple phrase "you are absent, I lack." Because it stages most effectively the drama of the epistolary gesture, the one-way exchange reveals the vanity of the letter, which is the "vanité de chercher à retenir avec des mots un être qu'on n'a pas su retenir avec les mains" (Bray 50). Writing becomes an inferior substitute for physical presence ... or does it?

Enter the Peruvian princess: I shall take as example of the complex "unilateral exchange" Mme de Graffigny's text *Lettres d'une Péruvienne*. I would like to advance a reading of this text that considers as primary the relationship between Zilia's unanswered letters and the solitude that she first fears and then embraces. Beyond the narrative possibilities that monophony provides (Zilia's desire to write intensifies as Aza's silence becomes more and more prolonged), I submit that Zilia's psychological evolution from dependence to independence may be read allegorically as a kind of *mise en scène* of artistic voice. In simpler terms, Zilia is above all a writer and her letters are an exploration of literary vocation. The seclusion that she first regrets and later covets becomes closely linked to the preservation of her art. When her autonomy appears to be threatened (by Aza and/or Déterville), so does her art. In this context Aza's silence and absence, as well as Déterville's "restraint," grant Zilia the "room"–both the physical space and the psychological freedom–to write. In this context the obstacle (Aza's absence) is actually desired and the illusory (and therefore perfect) "contact" achieved in writing is preferred to actual physical reunion. Paradoxically it is the removal of Aza as *un bel obstacle*–in other words, his presence–that threatens to obstruct Zilia's artistic growth most seriously.

THE LETTER AS CARREFOUR

With Madame de Graffigny more than with other epistolary writers, I am led to think of the letter as a kind of intersection at which various forms of literary discourse "collide." *Lettres d'une Péruvienne* bears the imprint not only of political satire, *tableau de société*, and sentimental novel but also of the lyric and dramatic genres. It seems that Graffigny's talent was too original and supple to be contained within a single genre. Her use of the "unilateral exchange" in this text exploits the lyric voice since it privileges a *mise en scène du je*. More precisely, she employs distinct rhetorical figures such as simile and hyperbole:

> Ainsi que la rose tire sa brillante couleur des rayons du Soleil, de même les charmes que tu trouves dans mon esprit et dans mes sentiments ne sont que les bienfaits de ton génie lumineux.... (Letter 2, 261)

> [J]e me représente le spectacle agréable de nos Vierges rassemblées ... telles que dans un jardin les plus brillantes fleurs tirent un nouvel éclat de la symétrie de leurs compartiments. (Letter 2, 263)

The figures of speech quoted above reflect the *style oriental* popular in the eighteenth century; as Nancy K. Miller points out in her book *Subject to Change*, this figuration in *language* may ultimately be read as Graffigny's attempt to address "woman's *identity* as a problem of figuration" (135, my emphasis). As I shall illustrate, Zilia's complex identity depends upon solitude, for it is solitude that allows for autonomy.

Along with figural language one finds innumerable examples of hyperbole, such as the following sentence chosen somewhat at random:

> O mon cher Aza! tous les tourments des âmes tendres sont rassemblés dans mon coeur: un moment de ta vue les dissiperait; je donnerais ma vie pour en jouir. (Letter 1, 260)

While tropes like hyperbole infiltrate the text with lyrical purpose, theatrical conceits shape the narrative events and allow Graffigny to inform her reader. The most pervasive theatrical borrowing in the text is Graffigny's treatment of dialogue: her use of prose transforms the traditional presentation of dialogue into reported dialogue. (It seems unlikely that Zilia would report such dialogues in letters to Aza; however, the author has already reacted to potential accusation of *invraisemblance* in her "Avertissement-prolepse"). Letters 23 and 31 typify the generic confusion between theatrical dialogue and epistolary prose:

> Ne vous offensez pas, Zilia, me dit-il; c'est le hasard qui m'a conduit à vos pieds, je ne vous cherchais pas ... [j]e vous ai aperçue, j'ai combattu avec moi-même pour m'éloigner de vous, mais je suis trop malheureux pour l'être sans relâche, par pitié pour moi je me suis approché, j'ai vu couler vos larmes, je n'ai

> plus été le maître de mon coeur, cependant si vous m'ordonnez de vous fuir, je vous obéirai. Le pourrez-vous, Zilia? vous suis-je odieux? Non, lui dis-je, au contraire, asseyez-vous, je suis bien aise de trouver une occasion de m'expliquer. Depuis vos derniers bienfaits ... N'en parlons point, interrompit-il vivement. Attendez, repris-je en l'interrompant à mon tour, pour être tout à fait généreux, il faut se prêter à la reconnaissance.... (Letter 31, 334)

If this dialogue were simply laid out on the page as in a theatrical manuscript, no changes would be necessary–actor and actress could immediately take their places on stage. By *burying* a theatrical discourse within the letter's solid blocks of prose, Graffigny is able to present the psychological subtleties of Zilia's changing relationship to Déterville.

Although Graffigny borrows from lyric and dramatic traditions, it is always in the interest of intensity of expression. Such intensity characterizes dramatic overture, and Zilia's opening letter echoes the exposition of the classical theatrical tradition. The text begins *in medias res*: Zilia has been torn from her beloved Aza and fears for his safety as well as for her own. The reader is led into Zilia's account of her abduction so quickly that she is bound to ignore, at least in the first reading, the fact that this same day was to be her wedding day: "ce jour horrible, ce jour à jamais épouvantable, devait éclairer le triomphe de notre union" (Letter 1, 258). Here we have an "underlayer" of a standard theatrical conceit: as the curtains open the spectator (reader) learns of a harmonious marriage that is supposed to transpire. True to classical dramatic convention, the text presents (albeit achronologically) a *moment d'équilibre* and its subsequent demise. Moreover, in the early morning hours before her capture Zilia *ran* to her *quipos*, "dans l'espérance qu'avec leur secours je rendrais immortelle l'histoire de notre amour et de notre bonheur" (258).

The image of the virgin bride hastening to record her happiness on paper suggests an awareness that the actual marriage and its consummation will bring an end to that happiness. Here is Rousseau's theory, uttered by a distraught Julie, that "le moment de la possession est une crise de l'amour" (24). Graffigny has her heroine abducted in the very hour of the promised communion, thereby "saving" Zilia from the crisis of possession. Although Zilia will continue to lament the *union brisée*, it seems ultimately that perhaps she does not mind so much. The deferred union still preserves the *possibility* of union, whereas actual presence is destined–at least in this story–to fail. Zilia's letters encode a subtle awareness of this paradox: desire is expressed metonymically through displacement–colored knots, the gaze, letters, foreign words–but never through physical union.

This displacement of desire becomes the means through which Zilia protects both her physical and psychological autonomy. Although Zilia repeatedly writes to her silent prince that she cannot continue without him, her actions–her life–reveal the reverse to be true. Carol Sherman points out that Zilia's ritualized plea for reunion paradoxically serves to frame an independent space of "exploration and discovery" ("Love's Rhetoric" 31). This space, which is always a space of *étrangeté*, is alternately represented as a physical space (France), a linguistic space (the French language), and a literary space (the letter).

CETTE DOUCE ERREUR

In her fourth letter, Zilia speaks of the "sweet error" of illusion that her writing affords:

> ces noeuds qui frappent mes sens, semblent donner plus de réalité à mes pensées; la sorte de ressemblance que je m'imagine qu'ils ont avec les paroles, me fait une illusion qui trompe ma douleur: je crois te parler, te dire que je t'aime ... cette douce erreur est mon bien et ma vie. (Letter 4, 270)

Here I believe is the explanation behind Zilia's feigned desire for reunion and her true desire that that reunion be deferred. Even in this early letter (she is still communicating with her *quipos*) Zilia articulates a preference for imagination over reality, for Art over life. She mentions that writing down her thoughts makes them more genuine and also proffers an illusion that lessens the pain of experience. Her oft-quoted phrase "je crois te parler" reveals that she prefers imaginary talk to actual talk. Although she claims elsewhere that Aza is her life (Letter 3), he is actually only the vehicle for her Art. It is Zilia's writing that is actually most important to her, and she does not deny it: "cette douce erreur est mon bien et ma vie"

(Letter 4, 270), "j'ai passé [mon] temps à m'entretenir avec toi: c'est tout mon bien, c'est toute ma joie" (Letter 13, 291).

Zilia's solitude is an artistic solitude: Aza's silence ultimately serves her art in that it allows her to place the imagined life above actual experience. He is, in short, Zilia's Muse. Now the pertinent aspect of the Muse is that he/she remains a mysterious, abstract source of artistic inspiration; Aza is just that. This explains why his physical presence paradoxically "makes impossible the fusion imagined in his absence" (Sherman "Love's Rhetoric" 31). Because the act of imagining aspires to perfection, it requires a blind spot and a lack: if the Muse becomes real, there can be no more art. In this context Aza's infidelity comes more as a blow to Zilia's art than to her life.

Zilia's happy transfer from Aza to Déterville represents a diffusion of desire, allowing Zilia the writer to conserve her art. As the object of passionate desire, Aza's position was too exclusive. Zilia had to rely too much on Aza as inspiration for her letters. By dissipating her desire into friendship, she adopts a sort of "economy of desire" that preserves Art by eclipsing the "destructive and tumultuous sentiments" of passion (Letter 41, 362). She speaks of friendship as "ce sage et doux lien," (346) explaining that "l'amitié ... partage sans crime et sans scrupule son affection entre plusieurs objets [tandis que] l'amour ... exige une préférence exclusive" (346). Since actual possession is bound to fall short of perfection it also announces the end of artistic possibility. If I have what I want, there is nothing to imagine–there is no Art. By refusing Déterville's desire for physical passion, Zilia sublimates her desire and assures its survival in further letters.

Solitude, Self-Possession, and the Artistic Voice

Critics such as Susan Lee Carrell and English Showalter have expressed dissatisfaction with the solitude chosen by Zilïa at the end of the text:

> [I]l lui manque la profondeur d'une véritable souffrance, ce qui rend pròblématique la vraisemblance psychologique du dénouement. (Carrell 92)

> [H]er love does not seem strong enough, nor her suffering deep enough, to justify the resolution she takes at the end, with the result that the novel appears unfinished. (Showalter 45)

This kind of uneasiness is not new, having inspired the various *Suites* that were written in an effort to close up this open work either "by marrying Zilia off ... or by converting her to Christianity" (Sherman 31). It is curious that current-day readers still find Graffigny's depiction of female independence baffling. Surely the matter of *vraisemblance* becomes moot once we consider the willing suspension of disbelief required by the reader all along. As for Zilia's suffering, I would argue that in between the stylized death-wish that closes Letter 39 and the collected opening tone of Letter 40 ("Je vis; le destin le veut, je me soumets à ses lois") there is a blank space and a silence begging to be read. Zilia herself refers to the temporal gap (of which the blank space is a sign) when she alludes to "la longue et accablante léthargie où me plongea le départ d'Aza" (Letter 40, 359). Although the (symbolic) death occurs offstage, it still occurs.

Zilia writes to her companion Déterville that upon emerging from the depression caused by Aza's appearance and departure, "le premier désir que m'inspira la nature fut de me retirer dans la solitude que je dois à votre prévoyante bonté" (359). If the reader has not become aware of Zilia's desire for solitude by now, she does in Letter 40. Zilia expresses *reconnaissance* to Déterville for having procured her a house–more importantly, a house containing a *cabinet* which from 1627 was designated as a room "où l'on se retire pour travailler." Déterville helps her to obtain a room of her own, a place to work and be alone. Zilia is delighted, relating to Aza

> Le seul endroit où je m'arrêtai fut une assez grande chambre entourée d'un grillage d'or, légèrement travaillé, qui renfermait une infinité de livres, de toutes couleurs, de toutes formes, et d'une propreté admirable; j'étais dans un tel enchantement, que je croyais ne pouvoir les quitter sans les avoir tous lus. Céline m'en arracha.... (Letter 35, 350)

It is in this space *à part*–a space allowing her contemplative solitude–that Zilia "arrives at writing as the expression of her being" (Sherman "Love's Rhetoric" 34). In contrast to the Peruvian Temple and the convent, which were spaces of *isolation* from self and society, her beautiful study is a voluntary space of seclusion where Zilia savors the delicious freedom of intellectual and emotional independence:

> L'avouerai-je? les douceurs de la liberté se présentent quelquefois à mon imagination, je les écoute ... [p]eut-être la fastueuse décence de votre nation ne permet-elle pas à mon âge l'indépendance et la solitude où je vis.... (Letter 40, 360)

AMI, AMANT: ADJUVANT(S), OPPOSANT(S)

By the end of the text, the reader knows that Zilia has "made it"–she has broken out of an economy of possession and dependence and has discovered–through the act of writing–"une connaissance ... de [s]a propre existence" (Letter 41, 362). In an age where young women were faced with the "choice" of becoming either a nun or a wife, Zilia has become an intellectual, a writer. How did she do it?

In order to answer this question I found it helpful to plot her development using Greimas's well-known *modèle actantiel*. That the narrative lends itself so readily to this model is further testament to the flexibility of the letter as literary form:

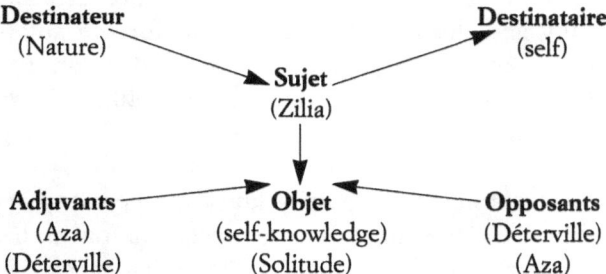

What this model allows me to observe is that the male characters in this text both aid and hinder Zilia in her journey toward selfhood. What Zilia needs to achieve self-understanding is the seclusion necessary if she is to write. On this point she is explicit, stating over and over that writing is "tout [s]on bien" and that she needs time alone (326).

Interestingly, Aza and Déterville trade places as they hover near (and far) throughout her quest. At first, Aza's role as "l'absent énigmatique" is beneficial to Zilia's progress. Not only does his faraway location motivate Zilia to recount her actions and express her thoughts in writing, it allows her to use him as a screen for Déterville's desire. Aza becomes the (usually non-existent) "boyfriend" to whom a woman can refer in an attempt to be left alone. Not unlike the dynamic between Wolmar and Saint-Preux in Rousseau's novel, Aza's existence exerts a constraint on Déterville and *deters* his attempts at possession. Being the gentleman that he is, Déterville does not overstate his amorous case until after Aza has betrayed the young princess. Affecting a sort of *flip-flop* between the role of *adjuvant* and *opposant*, Aza's marriage to *une belle Espagnole* coincides with a transformation from a role of assistance to one of hindrance. Because she can no longer use Aza as a screen, Zilia must resist Déterville's desire and possibly diffuse her own.

Déterville, too, acts both as helper and as threat to Zilia's quest for independence. Curiously, he helps to provide her with the material means to autonomy: he sells her golden throne and with it buys the country house complete with its study full of paintings and books. However alongside these actions he makes persistent claims to Zilia because he is in love with her. Letters 31 and 41 describe her very assertive refusal of passion and invitation of friendship: the point of crisis in the text is not Aza's betrayal, but instead the threat that this poses to her growing independence. After Aza announces his infidelity and departs, Zilia must fight for the autonomy to which she had unwittingly grown accustomed. By means of a verbal duel that is still going on when the text ends, Zilia exhorts Déterville to accept from her nothing beyond what she is able to give: her friendship.

As a writer, Mme de Graffigny knew the necessity of solitary work and took extraordinary pains to create a narrative that would depict its importance. The reading public's thirst for exotic tales as well as the fashion of epistolary writing came together in her text, allowing her to recount allegorically the "exotic" life of the woman writer from a first person point of view. Artistic voice, Graffigny knew, demands seclusion and self-possession. The true dilemma presented in *Lettres d'une Péruvienne* is the contemporary dilemma of "having it all." Even on her wedding day, Zilia was up early, "writing" in silk cords:

> A mesure que je travaillais, l'entreprise me paraissait moins difficile; de moment en moment cet amas innombrable de cordons devenait sous mes doigts une peinture fidèle de nos actions et de nos sentiments, comme il était autrefois l'interprète de nos pensées, pendant les longs intervalles que nous passions sans nous voir. (Letter 1, 258)

Had the wedding transpired there would have been no further occasion for Zilia to develop as a writer. By having her heroine abducted Graffigny devised an acceptable narrative through which she could depict the state of mind of a woman writer. Her ingenious narrative strategies for keeping Zilia alive and well–and writing–confirm the polyvalence of the letter. Her "radical" conclusion, which permits Zilia to live, choose her desires, and write them down, offers readers ways of being beyond closed obedience and submission.

II

BLANK SPACE AND THE EPISTOLARY
HORS-SCÈNE

In epistolary texts, each page presents alternating patterns of writing and of blank space. Because blank paper surrounds the epistles that comprise the narrative, it may be said to participate in the signifying process. Similar to poems, and in opposition to conventional novelistic form, empty space subverts the printed word and represents an inversion of language; ultimately, it signifies silence and absence. In this chapter I am interested in ways of *reading* the space that characterizes epistolary texts. In Chapter One I set forth an appreciation of the letter as a kind of hybrid genre located at the crossroads of dramatic monologue and prose poem. In epistolary writing,[1] interludes of silence infiltrate the printed page and separate one utterance from the next. In a different sense, these interludes connect the individual letters of an epistolary text much as the links of a chain do. *Les blancs* may therefore be said to divide but also to join the individual letters of an epistolary text. Because it both separates and unites, blank space in epistolary writing is equivocal and complex.

Jean Rousset and Janet Altman have acknowledged that *le blanc* is unique to epistolary writing:

> ... un blanc prend une signification; les parties muettes du livre entrent, elles aussi, dans la structure du livre. (Rousset *Forme* 84)

---

[1] Epistolary writing distinguishes itself from conventional prose texts because blank space creates "stops" or gaps between letters and sometimes within an individual letter. Because it incorporates blank space, it shares an affinity with poetic writing and dramatic texts. The process of reading poetry, letter-texts, or plays is altered by the need to "read" or navigate around or within blank paper. Blank paper inscribes silence as the supreme eloquence.

> ... the blank space between letters is as responsible for shaping the narrative as the letter itself. (Altman 171)

When I read Rousset's phrase "un blanc prend une signification," I ask "laquelle, lesquelles?" When Altman speaks of narrative shaping, I ask "how and to what effect?" In this chapter I shall provide possible answers to such questions.

In a general sense, blank space constitutes one half of that literary space defined by Blanchot as an intimate *point de rencontre* between writer and reader:

> Jamais le poète, celui qui écrit, le 'créateur,' ne pourrait du désoeuvrement essentiel exprimer l'oeuvre ... l'oeuvre est oeuvre seulement quand elle devient l'intimité ouverte de quelqu'un qui l'écrit et de quelqu'un qui la lit, l'espace violemment déployé par la contestation mutuelle du pouvoir de dire et du pouvoir d'entendre. (35)

Epistolary writing may be said to illustrate Blanchot's definition of literary space since it dramatizes so explicitly the exchange between *someone writing* and *someone reading*. The intimate space of exchange is counterbalanced by impersonal white space. The written word becomes the space of personal inscription—*le dire*—whereas blank space denotes a silence and an absence—*la parole tue*. The so-called empty space in epistolary texts creates a sense of impermanence and passage (recalling the letter's movement in space and time); it is also a silent space of reading and contemplation. As I shall demonstrate, the seemingly negligible *blanc* inscribes a sophisticated and often disconcerting *espace-autre* within the written text. Ultimately, I shall associate this poetic space with the Lacanian unconscious and with notions of perfection and death.

Blank Space as *le hors-scène*

My approach to the question of blank space in letter-texts begins with the question of genesis and ends with some reflections on reception: by this path of meditation I am interested in asking first *why* and then *how*. Why did the writer undertake to represent the epistolary exchange, and why did it become the narrative convention during the Enlightenment? What narrative and esthetic purposes might have been served in infiltrating lyrical prose with so-called empty space? How might contemporary readers effectively navigate the textual flux between letters and blank space? Is *le blanc* also to be read, or should it be skipped? And if it is to be read, how?

Concerning genesis, these silent interludes may be read as an evolution of the off-stage space in the theatrical tradition. My theory is that *le blanc* evolved out of this tradition in deference (whether genuine or feigned) to the dramatic tradition of the seventeenth century. Such deference may be construed as the writer's solution to the dilemma proposed by Georges May; I shall return to May's concept shortly. In Classical French theater (in Corneille and Molière, and especially in Racine), everything happens off-stage: battles are fought, loves won, lives lost.[2] The stage is a place of *re*action rather than action, a place of speech and not deed. Similarly, plain whiteness operates as a kind of *off-page* imaginary space. All actions in epistolary writing have either already happened or are yet to occur; the letter merely recounts events, provides psychological reactions, and speculates as to the future. Like the unseen space beyond the dimensions of the stage, blank space in letter-texts is above all a space of paradox: it is the space of high actions, unseen.

Blankness is the screen behind which the *event* occurs. Now the paradox of this type of anti-space is that it functions more effectively than the linguistic (or visual) sign. It would seem that the gap between signifier (blank paper) and signified (high action) could not be greater; however, *le blanc* signifies action and *le hors-scène* designates a space of union and dissolution, love and death. To put it another way, the linguistic sign refers to an absence, stating a negation, whereas the surrounding whiteness *evokes* that absence positively. Similarly, the imaginary space beyond the stage communicates so intensely because it is never represented through visual or corporal signs. Like the off-stage space, the textual blank is a manifestation of the absence of the referent. It is appropriate here that the manifestation negates both sense and presence.

---

[2] Corneille's theater is generally thought to reflect the baroque esthetic more than Classical taste. Nevertheless, the famous on-stage slap that occurs in Act I, scene III of *Le Cid* provoked much controversy and shocked the nascent Classical sensibility. For the most part, Corneille situates the major actions of his story in the imaginary *hors-scène*.

In letter-texts blank space operates much like *le hors-scène* in Racinian tragedy. An example: Phèdre is never so present to the reader/viewer as she is in the moment preceding her first appearance on stage. Evoked by Oenone's words and demurring in the metaphorical *anti-chambre*, she is most present when she is unseen, an image hidden behind a screen of words:

> Hélas! Seigneur, quel trouble au mien peut être égal?
> La Reine touche presque à son terme fatal.
> En vain à l'observer jour et nuit je m'attache:
> Elle meurt dans mes bras d'un mal qu'elle me cache.
> (I, ii, 143-46)

Seemingly, it is through concealment that meaning is made: Phèdre's anguish is above all a response to the act of hiding her passion—*le mal caché*. Lyric Art seeks concealment in order to intensify meaning; the off-stage theatrical space and the poetic blank space manifest this occultation. While the body on stage and the word on the page are limited to an indexical meaning, pointing out an absence, the spatial void *enacts* that absence. Ironically, this spatial void achieves its own (anti)-language based on the inverse revelation of silence, the empty plenitude of the unseen.

In letters, blank paper operates as an inscription of a spatio-temporal void, *un espace-autre* where all action paradoxically takes place. A well-known example is the death of Julie in Rousseau's novel: while the tenth letter of Book Six (authored by Claire) recounts the death, the preceding off-page white space *evokes* it. The letter's opening lines merely recount the trace of a passage beyond any narration:

> C'en est fait, homme imprudent, homme infortuné, malheureux visionnaire! Jamais vous ne la reverrez ... le voile ... Julie n'est ... (535)

Claire's words tell Saint-Preux (and the reader) "you will never see her again," but the blankness manifests the ineffability of the fact. Claire's broken discourse functions like a veil; the fragmented sentences—*... le voile ... Julie n'est ...*—transform language into a transparent material, revealing blankness as the absolute articulation of death.

Because its absolute silence evokes—seemingly makes present—the absence of the referent, blank space may be said to operate paradoxically as both refusal and communion. It is a refusal in the sense that it negates and inverts the linguistic economy absolutely: it is not a sign of something absent, but rather *is* absence. In this sense it is a space of death. However, there is a paradox: white paper effects a communion even as it declares most completely the gap between word and thing. The negation of the sign entails the removal of discrimination and difference from the signifying process; as a result, all meanings are possible because none is singled out. In this sense blankness is a space of perfection. To borrow a line from Wallace Stevens, the blank paper that surrounds letters and poems is a manifestation of "nothing that is not there and the nothing that is" ("The Snow Man" 10).

THE OFF-PAGE SPACE OF CHANGE

The blank space between letters constitutes its own literary space. The example I gave above—the death of Rousseau's heroine Julie—is a particularly intense manipulation of white space. Nonetheless, *le blanc* generally operates as an *off-page* space of passage and change, particularly in monophonic texts where there is no possibility of third-person narration or of multiple focalization. As in the dramatic tradition, the letter merely recounts actions that occur off-page: encounters, marriages, betrayals, deaths. Examples of this space of change may be seen in Graffigny's *Lettres d'une Péruvienne*, Charrière's *Lettres de Mistress Henley*, and Riccoboni's *Lettres de Mistress Fanni Butlerd*.

In the *Lettres d'une Péruvienne*, blank space twice denotes an encounter with death. In her early correspondence, Zilia writes to Aza of her capture and confesses that despair is causing her to contemplate suicide; the reader is supposedly led to believe her death is near. Her letter ends with the rhetorical device of aposiopesis, which Webster defines as "a sudden breaking off of a thought ... as if one were unable or unwilling to continue":

> Que la mer abîme à jamais dans ses flots ma tendresse malheureuse, ma vie et mon désespoir.

> Reçois, trop malheureux Aza, reçois les derniers sentiments de mon coeur, il n'a reçu que ton image, il ne voulait vivre que pour toi, il meurt rempli de ton amour. Je t'aime, je le pense, je le sens encore, je le dis pour la dernière fois ... (Letter 6, 274)

Reading like an elegant prose poem, the closing lines of Letter 6 drop off into silence. In the gap or non-narration between Letters 6 and 7 Zilia attempts suicide. The princess refers to but does not recount her near death in the opening lines of Letter 7:

> Aza, tu n'as pas tout perdu; tu règnes encore sur un coeur; je respire. La vigilance de mes surveillants a rompu mon funeste dessein, il ne me reste que la honte d'en avoir tenté l'exécution. Je ne t'apprendrai point les circonstances d'un projet aussitôt détruit que formé. Oserais-je jamais lever les yeux jusqu'à toi, si tu avais été témoin de mon emportement? (274)

In this paragraph the reader learns that Zilia made an attempt on her life and that this grave *emportement* has left her changed. Whereas in her letter Zilia conceals rather than reveals—*je ne t'apprendrai point*—the blank space, in saying nothing, tells the story of her symbolic death. The interruption between these two letters encodes an omission more expressive than any narration. Graffigny employs the same narrative strategy near the end of her text with equal success: the whiteness that separates Letter 39 from Letter 40 may again be read as an off-page, circular passage from life to near-death and back again. By this time Zilia has changed *destinataires* and is now writing not to the *trop malheureux Aza* but instead to Déterville, her *trop généreux ami*:

> Ne cherchez point, Monsieur, à surmonter les obstacles qui vous retiennent à Malte pour revenir ici. Qu'y feriez-vous? Fuyez une malheureuse qui ne sent plus les bontés que l'on a pour elle, qui s'en fait un supplice, qui ne veut que mourir. (358)

> Rassurez-vous, trop généreux ami, je n'ai pas voulu vous écrire que mes jours ne fussent en sûreté, et que moins agitée je ne puisse calmer vos inquiétudes. Je vis; le destin le veut, je me soumets à ses lois. (359)

The blank space that simultaneously divides and joins these two letters evokes Zilia's passage from languishment to life. Now while Zilia's hyperbolic language is at times both precious and tedious, the language of *le blanc* is not. Mme de Graffigny ingeniously framed her epistolary narrative with two instances of symbolic death, evoked by blank space and by its language of omission.

The passage from life to death, whether real or symbolic, is not the only kind of action evoked in epistolary writing by white space. Blanks in the manuscript stand in for most actions, from a slip on the sidewalk in winter (Charrière's *Lettres neuchâteloises*) to a (seemingly) joyous marriage (Riccoboni's *Lettres de Milady Juliette Catesby*). Without exception, however, all high action in epistolary fiction takes place off-page: Saint-Preux and Julie kiss, Clarissa is raped, Madame de Tourvel succumbs, Fanni Butlerd is betrayed. To grasp the off-page event demands imaginative work on the part of the reader, who must envision in her own mind the scenes recounted on the page. Before turning my full attention to the question of reception, I shall develop the rapport between *le hors-scène* and epistolary blank space.

THE STAGE AND THE PAGE

I have proposed that the silent interruptions in epistolary texts evolved out of the theatrical tradition of seventeenth-century France, which in turn was the product of the Classical doctrine. During the reign of Louis XIV, Classical notions of decorum, understatement, and the three unities necessarily shaped the playwright's intent. Racinian tragedy is generally understood to epitomize Classical doctrine and Mme de Lafayette's novel *La Princesse de Clèves* is often regarded as a transposition of Classical tragedy into prose. My supposition is that epistolary writing absorbed many aspects of the Classical doctrine and rejected others. With the death of Louis XIV in 1715 came the slow demise of Classicism as an absolute esthetic. The legacy of this esthetic persisted into the next century nevertheless.

The eighteenth-century novelist may have adapted certain theatrical conventions to his or her prose works in an attempt to uplift public opinion of the novel as literary genre. Although the art of spectacle was coming under attack,[3] theater still enjoyed consider-

---

[3] Rousseau's *Lettre à d'Alembert sur les spectacles*, written in response to d'Alembert's article "Genève" and published in 1758, condemns the art of spectacle on the grounds of immorality. This publication effected a definitive rift between Rousseau and Diderot and incensed Voltaire.

able favor and was immensely popular at all social levels. By transposing dramatic conceits into novelistic form, the writer may have succeeded in safeguarding his or her work against censure or ridicule. Indeed, it is probable that the generic hybrid evolved as a solution to the dilemma of the Enlightenment artist as stated by Georges May:

> Fallait-il satisfaire les partisans d'une littérature d'édification morale, embellir donc la nature humaine en la peignant, l'idéaliser, et tomber, ce faisant, dans l'irréel et l'invraisemblable? Ou fallait-il, au contraire, représenter la nature humaine telle qu'elle était, et donc, dans la mesure où le réalisme est à l'art ce que le cynisme est à la morale, tomber dans l'immoralité? (102)

It seems that the way out of this dilemma, which May sums up with the binary opposition *réalisme/moralisme*, was to create a literature *à mi-chemin*, one that might represent human experience faithfully while still embellishing human nature. While the evolving novel tended to emphasize both material and psychological realism (one may cite a range of novelists from Lafayette to Diderot to Laclos), theatrical writing offered itself as a source of embellishment through exoticism (Voltaire's *Zaïre*), "lost-and-found" identities (Diderot's *Le fils naturel*, Graffigny's *Cénie*) and intricate masking and role-play (the theater of Marivaux).

Certain critics have already commented on the practice of dramatic borrowing in epistolary fiction. In Chapter One I observed that the dialogues recounted by Zilia in her letters to Aza read like dramatic dialogue transposed into prose. Jean Rousset has pointed out the affinity between theatrical and epistolary texts: "[d]ans le roman par lettres—comme au théâtre—les personnages disent leur vie en même temps qu'ils la vivent" (*Forme* 67). In addition, Janet Altman has written convincingly of the role of the absent *amie* in epistolary texts, identifying it as an evolution of the theatrical *confidente*.[4] Adding to this scholarship, I submit that the prevalence of blank space in epistolary texts may be interpreted as a textual manifestation of the imaginary *hors-scène*.

---

[4] In Chapter Two of her book *Epistolarity* Altman demonstrates how "[t]he confidante that the letter novel appropriated from classical theater is exploited in particular ways in narrative" (47).

In epistolary writing, the page becomes a private stage upon which a woman or man appears, speaks, and leaves. Like the stage, the page is a place not of action but of reflection. By transposing the off-stage theatrical space onto the blank page, the writer was able to allude to so-called improper actions without representing them. This technique allowed the writer to play with illusion and thereby maintain decorum without sacrificing the need for realistic imitation. A well-known example of this kind of narrative allusion/illusion is the report of Julie's miscarriage in *La Nouvelle Héloïse*: it is difficult to grasp because Rousseau buried it within a post script following Julie's description of her father's violent rage:

> P.-S. –Après ma lettre écrite, j'ai passé dans la chambre de ma mère, et je me suis trouvée si mal que je suis obligée de venir me remettre dans mon lit: je m'aperçois même ... je crains ... Ah! ma chère, je crains bien que ma chute d'hier n'ait quelque suite plus funeste que je n'avais pensé. Ainsi tout est fini pour moi; toutes mes espérances m'abandonnent en même temps. (Letter 63, 121)

Just as Julie's bodily existence is denied to her by those around her, her confidential post script is separated from the body of the preceding letter by blank space. Functioning like *le hors-scène*, *le blanc* becomes the abstract space of excess, the screen behind which Julie bleeds.

Dans cette béance, il se passe quelque chose

The words above are Lacan's, uttered during one of his seminars in 1964. The gap–*béance*–in this context is his metaphor for the unconscious. In this seminar, entitled "L'inconscient freudien et le nôtre," he outlines one of the primary concepts of his psychoanalytic theory: that the unconscious is structured like a language (23). He explains how Freud drew close to this supposition without ever stating the concept in succinct terms:

> L'inconscient de Freud n'est pas du tout l'inconscient romantique de la création imaginaire. Il n'est pas le lieu des divinités de la nuit ... [à] tous ces inconscients ... ce que Freud oppose, c'est la révélation qu'au niveau de l'inconscient il y a quelque chose en

> tous points homologue à ce qui se passe au niveau du sujet—ça parle, et ça fonctionne d'une façon aussi élaborée qu'au niveau du conscient, qui perd ainsi ce qui paraissait son privilège. (27)

As I think about possible ways of reading blank space in epistolary texts, I find myself resorting to some of the same spatial metaphors used by Lacan to describe his conception of the unconscious. Turning my attention to the question of reception, I shall examine the Lacanian notions of the boundary line or limit, as well as his image of the veil, in order to identify *le blanc* as a kind of emblem of the unconscious. The general affinity between Lacan's unconscious and the textual blank is that both *speak* paradoxically and intricately, by announcing their silence and revealing their occultation.

First, the gap. Lacan employs the word (and in fact borrows it from Kant) in an effort to grasp the nature of the unconscious (23). Without ever defining it completely, he speaks of the gap as "quelque chose de l'ordre de l'inconnu," as "cette zone des larves," and as "[un] nombril des rêves," (25-26). For him the unconscious is above all a non-realized force that reveals itself as absent (36). It is a silence that tells, a shadow that shows. It can only make itself known; it cannot be known. The unconscious is an inscription that takes place before any experience (20), existing before linguistic cognition and residing beyond its horizons. Indeed, in the context of both *le blanc* and the unconscious, the gap is the unseen place of high action—*le hors-scène*.

I have already discussed how the blank space between the individual letters of an epistolary text functions as a gap in narration—a gap where, paradoxically, everything happens. In addition, I have contrasted the linguistic sign, which is a mark or trace that *masks* or covers an absence, with *le blanc*, which *enacts* or evokes pure absence. In a Lacanian context, blankness is the place of non-narration. Here it is important to note that this silent place is not devoid of language; rather, it constitutes its own language, encoding an inverse plenitude of silence and an absence of sense. As the unconscious is to the conscious, so blank space is to the printed word: both are imaginary spaces, "ni être, ni non-être, c'est du non-réalisé" (Lacan 32).

Writing is a realization of a thought made concrete and set down on the page. Once my thought is written down, it is realized, and in being realized it finds its limit or end. Artistic expression demands this realization and this limit, and yet it longs for its own unexpressed silence or non-existence. Speaking of desire (which is to speak of *écriture*) Lacan suggests that "le désir, lui, trouve son cerne, son rapport fixé, sa limite, et c'est dans le rapport à cette limite qu'il se soutient comme tel...." (32). Now blank space in a printed text delineates a boundary, and it is in relation to blank space that writing finds its limit. Poetic writing begins by breaking a silence and ends by circling back to meet it again. There is an anxiety to this final encounter, and so epistolary convention dictates rituals of closure through the use of certain *formules de politesse*.

Like poetic and dramatic writing, epistolary writing ceaselessly redraws and then erases a boundary or edge: this edge is blank space. The letter, the dramatic text, and the poem all investigate silence as the limit of writing; this investigation is what lends these discourses their sophistication. Lacan states that desire sustains itself by testing out its own limits; I have equated desire with writing and identified those modes of discourse that carry within them their own silence. The silence that surrounds the poem, the blank that simultaneously joins and divides one letter from the next, the off-stage imaginary space of perfection and death–all are forms of writing that not only locate their own limit but wed it, as Persephone weds the god of Death.

How Fragile Are the Veils of the Unconscious

The veil differs from the boundary in that it is fluid, floats, admits to *le flou*. Lacan employs both spatial metaphors in an attempt to understand the unconscious. It is ironic that he describes the language of the unconscious as being "inaccessible ... à la localisation spatio-temporelle, et aussi bien à la fonction du temps" (33). He is using spatial metaphors to ascertain the nature of a force beyond conceptions of time and space. The unconscious surely cannot be located or measured–it is an epiphenomenon hinted at by language, laughter, desires, dreams. The veils, Lacan says, are fragile: we see through the words to the whiteness of the page, we understand the meaning of that dream, we know the laugh to be a mask. The fragility of language is the delicacy of the veil–Lacan speaks of the latter in order to describe the unconscious. The veil creates a communion between absence and presence since it both reveals and conceals. The unconscious, too, *speaks* by revealing itself as absent (Lacan 36).

During the eighteenth-century, the lyric impulse announced its own silence by veiling itself with letters of love and death. I have proposed that the lyric voice, which appeared to be suppressed in the name of epistemological and scientific progress, in fact *shows up* in the epistolary texts written during this period. Lacan's two spatial metaphors of the unconscious–the boundary line and the veil–serve to illustrate the nature of post-classical lyric.

Elisabeth Bronfen has astutely observed that "[l]ike an aesthetic order, a social order is constituted by virtue of what it seeks to evade" (215). Similarly, Lacan writes that desire sustains itself by locating its own boundary or limit (32). During the seventeenth century, the lyric became a kind of "off-limits" space or *terrain vague* toward which the artist strayed but could not stay. During the eighteenth century, the lyric remained suppressed in the societal unconscious, but it functioned more like Lacan's veil. This function is one of partial revelation and simultaneous concealment–*la transparence infranchissable*. Encoding an alternation between language and silence, mimesis and poesis, epistolary writing inscribes itself as a gesture of passage or trace and presents blank silence as an imaginary space of perfection and death.

III

THE SHORT TEXT: *INACHÈVEMENT*

What is the meaning of the word *novel?* Why are eighteenth-century French epistolary texts given that label? How do readers grasp narrative development in a short (thirty- to fifty-page) epistolary text? What is the relationship between brevity and poeticity? To what extent does the lyrical letter differ from a prose poem? These are the questions I undertake to explore and answer in the present discussion. In so doing, I shall propose that to call all epistolary narratives *novels* diminishes the possibilities for reader reception, particularly with regard to the short letter text.

Because the letter-form privileges the first-person singular and the use of the present tense, it runs counter to contemporary definitions of the novel. In addition, many epistolary *novels* (including the urtext of French epistolary writing, Guilleragues's *Lettres portugaises*) are in fact very short. In these shorter texts, moreover, the epistolary strategies of indeterminacy, open-endedness, and introversion appear to be intensified. For this reason, the short text—often consisting only of five or six letters—requires in my view new theoretical interpretations of epistolary genesis and reception. By renaming them *letter-texts* I aim to describe a literary space characterized by lyric purpose and by a lack of closure.

I am identifying the short letter-text as a polyvalent form in which seemingly disparate discourses intersect. Here my thinking is inspired by Tzvetan Todorov's *Introduction à la littérature fantastique*: in this work Todorov argues for the generic complexity of *le conte* and *la nouvelle* and identifies in these forms a kind of esthetic enmeshment of poetic code and narrative voice. Todorov's study of the fantastic expanded the reader's horizon of expectation such that no one reading today would conflate Balzac's *Le Chef d'oeuvre inconnu* with his novels, or call Gautier a novelist. Readers of short epistolary texts stand to benefit from a similar shift in reception.

By considering the unique qualities of the short text, it is possible to ascertain the letter's influence upon the literary form that seeks to express the ideal "union of opposites" (Todorov 61): *le poème en prose*. The epistolary qualities of brevity, open-endedness, and fragmentation establish a link between the fictitious letter and the prose poem. As the vehicle of lyricism during the French Enlightenment, the letter may be read not only as a textual "ancestor" of the prose poem, but as a kind of prose poem in its own right.

CECI N'EST PAS UN ROMAN

To enter into the question, I offer some historical definitions of the novel. In his essay *De l'origine des romans* (1670) Huet set down his understanding of the word:

> Autrefois, sous le nom de Romans, on comprenait, non seulement ceux qui étaient écrits en prose, mais plus souvent encore ceux qui étaient écrits en vers ... [m]ais aujourd'hui l'usage contraire a prévalu, et ce qu'on appelle proprement Romans sont des fictions d'aventures amoureuses, écrites en prose avec art, pour le plaisir et l'instruction des lecteurs. (2-3)

Huet establishes his definition through exclusion: although novels used to be written both in prose and in verse, *today* (1670) only the work of prose may be called a novel, "pour être conforme à l'usage de ce siècle" (3). This act of defining through limitation typifies the Classical esthetic to the extent that it shuns excess and ambivalence: Huet carves his definition like a statue.

Nearly a century later, de Jaucourt composed a definition of the novel and published it in Diderot's *Encyclopédie*. His definition demonstrates a greater concern for content over form: where Huet advocated the importance of artful prose, de Jaucourt cares more for moral purpose:

> Roman, s.m. (Fictions d'esprit), récit fictif de diverses aventures merveilleuses ou vraisemblables de la vie humaine; le plus beau

> roman du monde, *Télémaque*, est un vrai poème à la mesure et à la rime près ... les *romans* écrits dans ce bon goût [he has just praised Richardson and Fielding] sont peut-être la dernière instruction qu'il reste à donner à une nation assez corrompue pour que toute autre instruction lui soit inutile. (quoted in Charpentier 159-60)

What I observe in this definition is the equivalence established between novel and poem: *Télémaque* is called both *le plus beau roman* and *un vrai poème*. Where Huet insisted upon the generic purity of the novel–no verse allowed–de Jaucourt's defining language allows for a generous conflation between novel and poem. This shift reveals the extent to which the eighteenth-century philosopher moves away from Boileau's negative equation–*rien n'est beau que le vrai*. With the Enlightenment, the ideal to which the novelist can aspire is identified as a poetic one.

Indeed, in his *Prospectus de l'Encyclopédie* Diderot includes novels as a part of his vast *mappemonde* of human knowledge. Undoubtedly inspired by John Locke in England and by Galiani in Italy, Diderot maps an outline of human understanding and calls it his "système figuré des connaissances humaines." He identifies three "principal faculties" through which human beings attain understanding: memory, reason, and imagination. Memory leads to historical knowledge, reason leads to philosophy, and imagination creates poetry. The novel, says Diderot, is but another form of poetry, *la poésie narrative*:

> Nous n'entendons ici par poésie que ce qui est fiction ... il peut y avoir versification sans poésie, & poésie sans versification.... (117)

From "artful prose" to "narrative poetry," the novel underwent a substantial shift in perception as philosophers questioned the esthetic legacy of Classicism. Two centuries later, philosophers are still tackling the same questions of poetics, comparing poetry to hedgehogs (Derrida) and peacocks (Johnson) and asking "if poetry is not verse, what is it?" (Todorov "Poetry" 60).

A consideration of contemporary reception reveals that although twentieth-century readers embrace notions such as the self-referentiality of all literature and the death of the author, many still tend toward categorical *naming* as a method of understanding literary texts. We want to distinguish between novel and poem, we want to be clear on what happened at the end, we want to erase process and finish the chapter before we turn off the lamp and go to sleep. The desire for coherence, I believe, has led readers of epistolary literature to lump all epistolary texts under the heading of *novel*. Whether the text in question is some six hundred pages (*La Nouvelle Héloïse*) or a mere thirty-six (*Lettres portugaises*), it is called a *roman par lettres*.

In my readings on epistolary fiction I have found no mention of the distinct characteristics of the short epistolary text. The Flammarion anthology (1983) is a compilation of texts ranging from the twenty-five page *Lettres de la Grenouillère* to the comparatively lengthy *Lettres d'une Péruvienne* (one hundred and thirteen pages): all of the texts are referred to as novels. In their introduction to the new 1993 edition of Mme de Charrière's *Lettres de Mistress Henley publiées par son amie*, Philip and Joan Hinde Stewart refer to this forty-five page text as a "short novel" (xi) but later eliminate the modifier, calling it simply a novel and referring to Charrière's other works (all relatively short) as novels (xvi). In addition, the jacket copy to the slim volume refers to the work as "among the most brilliant novels written in French during the eighteenth century." On the back of the MLA edition of Graffigny's *Lettres d'une Péruvienne* appears Janet Altman's statement that the text is "one of the three or four most influential novels of the French Enlightenment."

When it is applied to short texts, the appellation of novel is more than a misnomer–it seems to betray the very esthetic that shaped the period in which the texts were written. Contemporary critical viewpoints seem less flexible than those of the eighteenth century: let us recall that Diderot equated fiction with *poésie* and additionally instructed readers that the novel was a narrative form of poetry. My suspicion is that the misapplication of the term *novel* derives specifically from an erroneous sense that these female-authored texts are inadequate, that they will not "make it" into the canon unless they are called novels.

In *Tender Geographies*, Joan DeJean demonstrates that "in France, the novel was a feminist creation" (5). Her skillful analysis of the evolution of novels reveals the enormous contributions of women writers during the seventeenth and eighteenth centuries. Her argument centers around the idea of a genre *in-the-making*, as she asserts that "feminist ideas played a crucial role in the development of the French novel" (5). Building on DeJean's reaffirmation of a female tradition, I aim to show that to call short letter texts *novels* shortchanges this newly-delineated female tradition. When twentieth-century readers apply notions of the *nineteenth-century* novel to the more varied, eclectic forms of the eighteenth century, we miss out on the originality of epistolary writing. DeJean mentions, for example, that Lafayette's *Zayde* may be seen as a "miniaturization of the form known at the period as the *nouvelle*" (5). My interest in the *short epistolary text* owes much to DeJean's fine-tuned appreciation of the not-so-subtle differences between prose forms.

Let us consider contemporary definitions of the novel to see how they might be obstructing an understanding of the short text. According to Larousse, the word *roman* is defined as "une oeuvre d'imagination, constituée par un récit en prose *d'une certaine longueur*, dont l'intérêt est dans la narration d'aventures, l'étude de moeurs ou de caractères, l'analyse de sentiments ou de passions." Webster reiterates the exigency that the work be long, defining the novel as "*a relatively long* fictional prose narrative with a more or less complex plot or pattern of events, about actions, feelings, motives, etc. of a group of characters." In both instances, one of the novel's defining features is its relative length; a twenty-five or fifty page text therefore does not adhere to the definition. The monophonic letter-text, furthermore, does not present a group of characters, but instead a solitary female voice. While Larousse and Webster do not specify what is meant by "relatively long," it is safe to say that any text under one hundred pages does not fit the definition.

I sense that in an effort to introduce the fictional texts of the *épistolières* within the canon of French literature–an effort both justifiable and long overdue–feminist critics (both male and female) have been employing the term *novel* politically. When it is applied to the short letter-text, the label not only fails to describe the short text but also fails to reflect historical perceptions of narrative. In my view this misuse of the label *novel* as a feminist strategy ultimately eclipses esthetic concerns. The argument seems to run like this: if I compare Mme de Graffigny to a Montesquieu or to a Rousseau, her work will be accepted, read, and published. But that amounts to an encoding of the female voice within a male-driven norm. The danger in this gesture is that the specificity of the female voice will be subsumed through conformity, therefore effacing itself by canonical imitation.

The female-authored texts with which I am concerned differ from those written by men. Technically speaking, they are shorter, they employ monophony more often than male-authored texts, and above all they tend to resist closure. These qualities may be read as inscriptions of female experience, of difference and *différance*. By insisting on ways in which they are *different* from the canonical, male-authored novels, I hope to inspire interest based not on generic contiguity with the accepted canon but rather on originality and generic specificity.

THE OPEN WORK

The originality of the female-authored letter-text is to be found in its brevity and its refusal of closure. The *épistolière* generally writes a short, open work. In this sense she remains closer to the model of all modern epistolary writing: *Lettres portugaises*. Earlier I referred to the unease that Mme de Graffigny inspired by placing her protagonist outside of societal and narrative codes. An equally unorthodox ending is the final letter of Mme de Charrière's protagonist Mistress Henley. In her sixth and last missive to her ever-absent *amie*, Mistress Henley records the horror with which she realizes, fully and for the first time, the degree of indifference that governs her marriage to her *trop raisonnable mari*:

> [j'ai ressenti si fort] l'horreur de me voir si étrangère à ses sentiments, si fort exclue de ses pensées, si inutile, si isolée, que je n'ai pu parler ... je me suis évanouie ... [m]on âme ni mon corps ne sont dans un état naturel. Je ne suis qu'une femme, je ne m'ôterai pas la vie, je n'en aurai pas le courage; si je deviens mère, je souhaite de n'en avoir jamais la volonté; mais le chagrin tue aussi. Dans un an, dans deux ans, vous apprendrez, je l'espère, que je suis raisonnable et heureuse, ou que je ne suis plus. (45)

At the end of this short text, openness prevails over a sense of closure: there is an account of a symbolic death (*l'évanouissement*) mixed with the overtone of a possible suicide or literal death caused by anguish. In addition to the oscillation between living and dying there is insecurity as to whether the heroine will in fact carry her baby to term (*si je deviens mère*). The thematic ambivalence of a young pregnant woman contemplating suicide finds its echo on the level of rhetorical ambiguity: her prose is rendered serpentine through repetition (*si fort exclue ... si inutile, si isolée*), litotes (*mais le chagrin tue aussi*) and syntactic symmetries. Hovering between self-expression and self-effacement, Mistress Henley's final letter alludes to the possibility of another even as she calls her very survival into question. The letter both records the trace of experience and announces a death, and in this sense reads much like a lyric poem.

Writing on the epistolary texts of Graffigny and Charrière, Elizabeth MacArthur identifies the use of the present tense and the absence of an authoritative voice (or omniscient narrator) as factors impeding closure in the epistolary genre. MacArthur's analysis focuses on women's writing as feminist strategy and posits that the "devious narratives" of these *épistolières* resist the accepted destinies of literary heroines: marriage, the convent, death. On the level of esthetics, the deviance of epistolary writing–its inability to end–suggests linguistic disorder as well as political protest. One may say that the "unresolved error" (MacArthur 19) of the monophonic voice manifests itself as the semiotic: the letter as wandering signifier seeking a silent *destinataire*.

Epistolary writing never ends because each letter refers to the possibility of the next: letters cultivate a simulacrum of contact even as they depend upon separation in time and space. In contrast to the concrete sense of closure in both dramatic and narrative texts –typically achieved through marriage or death–epistolary closure "fails" to provide the sort of "retrospective illumination [that makes for a] plenitude of ending" (Brooks quoted in MacArthur 1). Indeed, it is safe to say that up until the twentieth century, much of the traditional canon portrays closure through the narrative turns of marriage and death. Moreover, it is often through control of the female body that such closure is achieved: one may cite the climactic deathbed scenes of Julie d'Etanges and Emma Bovary alongside the (seemingly) merrier nuptial scenes in the writings of Marivaux and Beaumarchais. Narrative closure often comes about by marrying the female character–thus controlling her body and its desires–or by destroying her altogether. In contrast, the *épistolière* often *equates* marriage with symbolic death (Charrière's *Mistress Henley*), thereby criticizing the institution, or dares to present solitude as an enviable state of being for a woman (Riccoboni's *Fanni Butlerd*, Graffigny's *Lettres d'une Péruvienne*). Here we may note the contrast with authors such as Laclos, who presented (in the figure of Mme de Merteuil) female autonomy as a threat to society.

On an esthetic level, the open-endedness of the epistolary text shows how all writing records signs and songs of experience even as it removes the writer from that which she wishes to record. The present moment fades before the page. This gap or vanishing between the lived moment and its capture on paper is what creates the impossibility of artistic ending. The vanishing that is never vanquished in epistolary writing is the same force that brings a poem into being while already condemning it as a *bel échec*. I am speaking here of the shadowy incommunicability of both letter and poem–the separation they confirm, their one-way errancy, the loneliness to which they both admit.

If during the eighteenth century the letter became what I call the vehicle of lyricism, then there must be a link between the letters of the eighteenth century and the poems of the following century. My thesis is that the prose poem, which flowered in the nineteenth century and indeed is thought to have originated then, owes much to the epistolary genre. The nature of this "unpaid debt" has not been adequately put forth. The reasons for this may have to do with the general disfavor that many critics have shown toward epistolary writing, such as English Showalter who criticizes the letter form as a technical "blind alley ... [weakened by] the bondage of the first person" (121).

At times the "blind alley" actually takes us where we want to go. The letter became an alley–*un aller*–for the lyric poet who wanted to break up *l'alexandrin* and render it more supple. Because it required the use of the first-person singular and the present tense, the letter provided the poet with the main coordinates of poetry without the limitation of the alexandrine line. The happy accident of the letter is that it diffused *l'expression du moi* into prose.

In the major studies on the prose poem (Caws and Bernard) the eighteenth century is credited with having influenced it only minimally. Critics generally concede that the concept of *sensibilité* had "something to do" with the lyric flowering of the nineteenth century, and passing reference is repeatedly made to the contribution of Rousseau. In her vast study entitled *Le Poème en prose de Baude-*

laire jusqu'à nos jours[1] Suzanne Bernard praises Rousseau's contributions to lyric voice, even citing the question that the author of the *Rêveries*[2] asked himself: "comment être poète en prose?" (29). In her "Aperçu historique" Bernard names the fictitious letter as a minor influence on the prose poem, whose major sources were the French prose translations of foreign verse-poetry:

> C'est dans les traductions que le public français du XVIIIe siècle a cherché, bien souvent, à contenter des aspirations poétiques qui ne trouvaient plus d'aliments dans les exercices purement formels des versificateurs; c'est par les traductions que les écrivains français ont fait les premiers essais de 'poèmes en prose,' différents et du roman et du poème épique. (24)

Among these prose translations of foreign verse Bernard cites as the most significant those Turgot made of Ossian in 1760 (25, 26). According to Bernard, while the *roman par lettres* did send "des ondes de lyrisme" into Enlightenment literature, it was prose translations that most effectively prepared the way for Baudelaire, Rimbaud and Mallarmé.

Bernard's thesis discounts the *original* contributions of poets such as Guilleragues, Diderot, Graffigny and Rousseau. It is one thing to translate and quite another to write original lyric prose; it seems clear that the romantic prose of Rousseau, Chateaubriand, and Aloysius Bertrand evolved from the latter. By identifying the fictitious letter as a primary rather than a secondary influence on the prose poem, an original tradition may be traced. *The Princeton Handbook of Poetic Terms* affirms the prose poem's indebtedness to original works written in France:

---

[1] The fact that Bernard begins her expansive study of the prose poem in France with Baudelaire has left unchallenged the critical view that experimentation between prose and verse was most innovative during the nineteenth century. This of course is untrue: Fénélon's *Télémaque*, Montesquieu's *Le Temple de Gnide* and Voltaire's philosophical discourses written in verse have all been cited as important instances of generic blending. Many other Classical and baroque narratives reveal generic ingenuity, such as d'Urfé's *L'Astrée*, Scarron's *Le Roman comique*, and Lafayette's *La Princesse de Clèves*.

[2] Bernard does not consider the importance of the *Rêveries*, which may themselves be read as letters from Rousseau to Society.

> The tendency is to consider Aloysius Bertrand the creator of the prose poem; his *Gaspard de la nuit* of 1842 is the first published collection of indubitable prose poetry... But the actual beginnings are in that 18th-century France where the Academy's rigid rules of versification were driving many a potential poet with a taste for individuality into prose. Thus came about works like Fénélon's poetic novel *Télémaque* (1699) and Montesquieu's prose pastoral *Le Temple de Gnide* (1725); these, and their many imitators, represent an approach, and encouragement, to prose poetry. (214)

It is significant that the origins of the prose poem are here said to be found even before the beginning of the period known as the Enlightenment. For over one hundred years, the blending of prose and verse remained locked in the minds of French writers like a dream deferred.

A consideration of esthetic affinity between the fictitious letter and the prose poem offers new possibilities for contemporary reader reception. To demonstrate the extent to which the fictitious letter complies to definitions of the prose poem, I shall undertake a comparison of a letter penned by Riccoboni with one of Baudelaire's prose poems.

According to the *Princeton Handbook*, the prose poem is distinguished above all by its brevity and by its encoding of sound patterns and images. It is defined as

> A composition able to have any or all features of the lyric, except that it is put on the page–though not conceived of–as prose. It differs from poetic prose in that it is short and compact, from free verse in that it has no line breaks, from a short prose passage in that it has, usually, more pronounced rhythm, sonorous effects, imagery, and density of expression. It may contain even inner rhyme and metrical runs. Its length, generally, is from half a page (one or two paragraphs) to three or four pages, i.e. that of the average lyrical poem. (214)

I would like to test two examples against this definition: the twenty-first letter of Madame Riccoboni's *Lettres de Mistress Fanni Butlerd* (1757) and the second of Baudelaire's *Petits poèmes en prose* that is entitled "Le Désespoir de la vieille" (1862). The two texts resemble each other thematically in that both record the thoughts of a woman forcibly separated from the object of her affections: Fanni longs for her lover and the anonymous *vieille* longs for the recognition of a child.

1)
          Mardi à minuit, au coin de mon feu

Je ne veux pas me coucher; non je ne le veux pas: je veux rester là. Je n'aime pas de mon appartement que l'endroit où je suis. Ma chambre est un pays étranger pour moi: je ne vous y ai jamais vu. Ici tout est vif, tout est riant, tout a reçu l'empreinte chérie: ce cabinet est mon univers. Mais, mon cher Alfred, vous êtes encore avec les autres: dans une heure, dans deux, peut-être, vous serez avec moi. Votre main, cette main que j'aime, tracera les pensées délicates de votre âme: elle m'apprêtera le plus grand des plaisirs. Qu'il est doux de porter ses regards sur les expressions tendres et passionnées d'un amant que l'on adore, de se répéter les noms flatteurs qu'il nous donne. Je suis donc votre maîtresse, votre chère maîtresse, votre amie, votre première amie; vous ne vivez point loin de moi: vous ne sentez votre existence, que lorsque l'instant où vous m'allez voir, approche. Quoi, c'est moi qui anime cette jolie machine? c'est le feu de mon amour qui lui donne et le mouvement, et la grâce avec laquelle elle me meut? Ah, dis-le moi cent fois, mille fois; dis-le moi toujours! Qu'il était aimable ce soir! N'avoir pas vu que cette femme était belle! N'avoir pas vu que moi! Ah que je vous aime! Je vous aime tant, que si vous étiez là ... Je vous aimerais trop. (28-29)

2)
          Le Désespoir de la vieille

La petite vieille ratatinée se sentit toute réjouie en voyant ce joli enfant à qui chacun faisait fête, à qui tout le monde voulait plaire; ce joli être, si fragile comme elle, la petite vieille, et, comme elle aussi, sans dents et sans cheveux.

Et elle s'approcha de lui, voulant lui faire des risettes et des mines agréables.

Mais l'enfant épouvanté se débattait sous les caresses de la bonne femme décrépitée, et remplissait la maison de ses glapissements.

Alors la bonne vieille se retira dans sa solitude éternelle, et elle pleurait dans un coin, se disant "Ah! pour nous, malheureuses vieilles femmes, l'âge est passé de plaire, même aux innocents; et nous faisons horreur aux petits enfants que nous voulons aimer!" (148)

What I notice in comparing these two texts is 1) the extent to which both conform to the definition of the prose poem and 2) the fact that of the two, Baudelaire's is the more prosaic–more prose than poem.

In order to illustrate this point I have plotted the two texts against the definition given above:

	short and compact	pronounced rhythm	sonorous effects	imagery	density of expression
Text 1 (Riccoboni)	x	x	x	x	x
Text 2 (Baudelaire)	x	x			x

This simple schema shows that Baudelaire's prose poem lacks two characteristics of the prose poem: sonorous effects and imagery. Of course this is my reading, and my stake in this comparison is by now apparent; still, it is hard to argue that "Le Désespoir de la vieille" employs imagery and sonority. In addition to the conspicuous absence of a *je*, Baudelaire's prose poem favors narrative technique over personal expression. Where Riccoboni's letter employs metaphor ("ma chambre est un pays étranger," "le feu de mon amour"), rhythmic effects ("tout est vif, tout est riant, tout a reçu") and sonorous effect ("vous ne vivez point loin de moi"), Baudelaire's prose poem employs third-person narration and is devoid of tropes.

The tendency of Baudelaire's prose poems toward narrative and anecdote has puzzled critics: simply put, they read too much like "ordinary" prose. Michel Beaujour concedes that with Baudelaire–considered to be the first true practitioner of the form–the poetry becomes subsumed by narrative purpose:

> [s]ome of them are ... obviously unpoetical according to lyrical norms (except in terms of length) ... [y]et there are no criteria which allow one to exclude such 'prosaic' and 'anecdotal' pieces from the canon of the prose poem. (42)

While one cannot exclude the major practitioner of this form, one can introduce and include other short texts into the canon of prose poems. Letters conform to the notion of the prose poem to an equal extent that the prose poem itself does not.

Michel Beaujour's reaction to the "overly prosaic" quality of Baudelaire is to admit that "brevity is the only component [of the prose poem] enjoying general pertinence within the canon" (42).[3] If the difference between prose and a prose poem comes down to one of brevity, then surely the fictitious letter of the French Enlightenment—with its obvious lyrical energy—may be read as a prose poem.

At this point a justifiable objection may be voiced: do not fictitious letters succeed and follow each other in a relation of narrative contiguity? In response I would argue that each letter can stand on its own, citing Altman's view that every letter becomes an autonomous text by virtue of the blank space that surrounds it (167) and that the individual letter is capable of "creating highly organized internal structures" (168). Moreover, Baudelaire's *Petits poèmes en prose* have been read (by Michel Butor) as a "poetic novel" and have been admired for expressing "unity in diversity" (Beaujour 43, 46). It is not too much to point out that three of Baudelaire's prose poems, like his famous preface, are written to a specific *destinataire* and therefore differ only imperceptibly from letters.[4]

CET IDÉAL OBSÉDANT

The blending of prose and verse may be said to represent an "obsessive ideal," to quote Baudelaire: Voltaire warned against this romantic attempt, Diderot stopped heeding the warning, and Rousseau achieved the ideal to some extent. The ideal is romantic in its very nature, seeking transcendence over difference and striving to unite the dissociated verbal realms of abstraction and narration. Romantic, too, in that every attempt is inspired by the impos-

---

[3] In an effort to counterbalance his reluctant concession that Baudelaire's prose poem is ultimately more prosaic than poetic, Beaujour opens a secondary discussion of the prose poem as a "revelation of Being," moving into a discussion of Mallarmé. He makes "no attempt ... to synthesize the two approaches" (40).

[4] The three prose poems are "La Corde (à Edouard Manet)," "Le Thyrse (à Franz Liszt)," and "Les Bons Chiens (à M. Joseph Stevens)."

sibility of the desire: letters err too much on the side of sentiment and the prose poem privileges telling over showing. Like the maiden Persephone who never picked the flower, prose and verse draw close but never truly commune.

Throughout the Enlightenment, the ideal of *le mélange des genres* remained necessarily a "dream deferred;" and if Derrida has taught us anything it is that deferred meaning–*différance*–is the motor-force driving language. I have suggested that the poetic letter of the eighteenth century may have brought the writer closer to the ideal mixing of poem and prose. The space of deferral–which is a space of *attente*, of anticipation, of potential energy–may draw closer to the desire than the kinetic moment of possession or release. Perhaps Rousseau, who had the idea(l) of the prose poem in the horizon of his mind, manifested the dream more fully than Baudelaire. The poem "written" in the mind is always superior to its shadow traced on paper.

What I have proposed is not a new taxonomy of generic categories but rather a move away from classification. I have argued that in calling a twenty-five or forty-five page epistolary work a *novel* critics are delineating a horizon of expectation that is perhaps too restrictive. Texts such as Guilleragues's *Lettres portugaises* (which has been called "the original French epistolary novel") and Charrière's *Lettres de Mistress Henley* (unremittingly referred to as a novel) simply do not adhere to definitions of the novel, be they historical or contemporary. By calling these short works letter-texts, readers might value more highly the degree to which they resist narrative conventions and embrace poetic invention.

PART II: THEMES IN EPISTOLARY LYRIC

IV

WRITING AS MOURNING: SUBSTITUTIONS OF PRESENCE IN RICCOBONI'S *LETTRES DE MISTRESS FANNI BUTLERD*

In Chapter Two I demonstrated how blank space inscribes significant gaps and eloquent silences within epistolary narratives, drawing the reader's gaze beyond the scene of writing. This subtle shift away from the sign and toward non-verbal systems of signification involves a *transport de sens* characteristic of metonymy.[1] In this discussion I shall demonstrate how pictorial representation and visual perception ultimately subvert the linguistic sign, effecting a metonymic displacement similar to the narrative operation of *le*

---

[1] See Janet Altman's book *Epistolarity* for interpretations of metonymy in epistolary writing (pages 19, 76, 82, and 186). Henri Suhamy defines metonymy by contrasting it with metaphor:

> Dans la métaphore, le transport de sens se fait par le moyen d'une ressemblance. Dans la métonymie le transport utilise la voie d'une relation.... (46)

In addition, *The Princeton Handbook of Poetic Terms* offers a lengthy definition of metonymy, portions of which are useful in the present context: metonymy is defined as

> a trope in which one word is substituted for another on the basis of some material, causal, or conceptual relationship ... [b]ecause metonymy and synecdoche involve some literal or referential connection between tenor and vehicle, they are often contrasted with metaphor, in which no such relationship is apparent ... Attempts to clarify or revise the metonymy-metaphor opposition as conceived by Jakobson and Lacan have taken several forms ... De Man [sees] metonymy not only as referential, but as contingent or accidental, in opposition to the pull toward unification of essences that underlies most uses of metaphor. (144)

These definitions inform my understanding of the portrait as synecdoche in Riccoboni's text. The portrait fulfills a referential function (it refers to a real person), yet it draws the observer's gaze away from the referent and toward the *copy*. Fanni relates not to the original but to a mimetic representation that offers her meaning based on contiguity.

blanc. The source for this discussion is Marie-Jeanne Riccoboni's text entitled *Lettres de Mistress Fanni Butlerd* (1757). This monophonic, epistolary work provokes my thinking about the rapport(s) between actual presence and another *symbolic* presence achieved in the phantom communication of words and pictures. Through a detailed examination of the role of the portrait in this text, I aim to show that Riccoboni's protagonist is above all an artist who creates *shadows of presence* in order to grieve a lover's absence and a brother's death. The portrait as copy or ersatz gaze will prove to be the primary element within a metonymic language of mourning in which the sum of partial, symbolic substitutes proves to be greater than the whole.

Regards Masculins, Écriture Féminine

Before presenting a reading of *Lettres de Mistress Fanni Butlerd* I offer my theoretical approach to this female-authored text. My interest in the feminine scopic economy–woman's gaze–stems from a dissatisfaction with certain aspects of poststructuralist feminist discourse, most notably the concept of *écriture féminine*. This notion inevitably posits feminine writing as a mode of expression that is *essentially* different from the writing of men. Such a line of reasoning relies upon a binary framework based on sexual difference. Although feminist critics such as Kristeva and Cixous identify certain male writers to be practitioners of feminine writing,[2] their assertions regarding the inextricable connections between woman's writing, the female body, and so-called feminine mystery ultimately return the woman artist to the esthetic dark continent of unintelligibility. Emblematic of this reduction are the following statements, written by Kristeva and Cixous respectively:

> [U]ne femme, cela ne peut pas *être*: c'est même pas ce qui ne va pas dans l'être.... J'entends donc par "femme" ce qui ne se représente pas, ce qui ne se dit pas, ce qui reste en dehors des nominations et des idéologies. (Kristeva 21)

---

[2] As examples of male practitioners of *écriture féminine*, Cixous names Jean Genet and Kleist ("Le rire de la Méduse" 42). Similarly, Kristeva aligns the "revolutionary" nature of Lautréamont, Mallarmé, and Artaud with the political characteristics of feminine writing.

> Il faut que la femme écrive par son corps ... plus que l'homme ... les femmes sont corps. Plus corps, donc plus écriture. (Cixous 48)

Now while these feminist critics claim to reject binary distinctions between masculine and feminine writing, they invariably conceptualize *écriture féminine* through notions of sexual difference and linguistic non-existence. For example, Kristevan discourse likens feminine writing to the notion of political (and poetic) revolution, stating with resignation that both are predicated upon momentary irruptions followed by an inevitable return to linguistic and sociopolitical hegemony. Cixous, moreover, speaks of the need to forge an antilogos-weapon–"[é]crire pour forger l'arme antilogos"–in order to bring about a return of the repressed feminine that will be utterly destructive: "[une] langue imprenable qui crève les cloisonnements, classes et rhétoriques, ordonnances et codes" (43, 48).

It is somewhat ironic that while certain feminists were doing violence to so-called male language, Jacques Derrida was off creating new possibilities within it. He appropriated the more successful aspects of post-structuralist and postmodern feminist discourse –namely, those of verbal play, multiplicity, and mobility–in order to create the cornerstone term of Deconstruction, *différance*. It is clear that *destruction* differs greatly from *deconstruction* and that the latter effaces binary oppositions rather than merely restating them with the terms reversed. Indeed, critics such as Derrida and Judith Butler have imagined and articulated a critical discourse that replaces the notion of categorization with a new conception of writing as deferred desire. By asking new questions, Judith Butler frees feminist discourse from the snare of essentialism by debunking the very notion of difference:

> I asked, what configuration of power constructs the subject and the Other, that binary relation between 'men' and 'women,' and the internal stability of those terms? What restriction is here at work? ... [d]oes being female constitute a 'natural' fact or a cultural performance? ... As a strategy to denaturalize and resignify bodily categories, I describe and propose a set of parodic practices based in a performative theory of gender acts that disrupt the categories of the body, sex, gender, and sexuality and occasion their subversive resignification and proliferation beyond the binary frame. (viii, x)

What Butler proposes is a new feminist approach requiring *resignification* rather than resignation: by showing that the notion of feminine writing is supported by the same binary opposition that it seeks to transcend, she reveals its speciousness. Rather than reinscribing the idea of woman as Other, which amounts to a recapitulation of the very identity feminists seek to surpass, Butler exhorts feminist critics to "get on with the task of politics" (ix). This task entails a subversion, since it disobeys systems of power in both language and society.

It is relevant that Butler employs the gaze in order to speak of the "trouble" she both courts and provokes. On the first page of her book *Gender Trouble* she rejects the conflation of femininity with mysterious unknowability and makes a claim for female agency (vii). The new female subject speaks directly in the uncompromising language of the eyes: she "inexplicably returns the glance, reverses the gaze ... and suddenly exposes [the] autonomy [of the masculine subject] as illusory" (vii). Female agency does not imply a 180-degree reversal wherein the woman names herself Subject and re-names the male Object. Instead, Butler reveals the subject-object opposition to be a linguistic and socio-political *construction* that loses its discursive and political power once we recognize it as such.

The principle of woman's "unanticipated agency" (Butler vii), which achieves expression not in body-words but in the gaze, finds its finest illustration with the Greeks. Greek myth relates that Actaeon, a great hunter, was out in the wild when he happened upon a clearing; here, in "the crystal water ... the goddess [Artemis] had let fall her garments and stood in her naked beauty on the water's edge" (Hamilton 374). Actaeon's eyes seized upon this sight, but to his surprise Diana met and held his gaze: in hers, the hunter saw spiritual strength and self-possession. Not once did she smile; neither did she blush or avert her eyes. The myth relates how

> [t]he offended divinity gave not a thought to whether the youth had purposely insulted her or had come there in all innocence. She flung into his face drops from her wet hand and as they fell upon him he was changed into a stag. Not only outwardly. His heart became a deer's heart and he who had never known fear before was afraid and fled. (Hamilton 374)

This ancient narrative allows readers to imagine a pre-ontological moment when binary constructions did not govern word and deed. Artemis's acts of confrontation and retribution subvert the paradigm wherein the passive female is subjugated to the possessive male gaze.[3] As such, the myth may be readily associated with Judith Butler's postmodern theory of gender trouble. Both refuse the validity of subject-object oppositions and envision instead a certain relational fluidity. By relational fluidity I mean that individual identity and interaction undergo both fluctuation and transformation: Artemis is the object of Actaeon's gaze but she is equally a subject, changing the hunter into the hunted. The mortal and the goddess are neither subject nor object but rather both at once, parts of a whole, their gazes forever encircling in a plural economy of desire.

Of course the time of divine mingling is long past, if it ever was. However, when considered in a more abstract sense, the ancient concept of divine agency within earthly life may be said to illustrate the relational fluidity that has become so important to postmodern feminist inquiry. To be succinct: the Greek dream of metamorphosis and mobility finds its echo in Deconstruction and in postmodern feminist discourse. Roberto Calasso has proposed that metamorphosis was the foremost principle of Greek experience and thought, writing that "[f]orms would become manifest insofar as they underwent metamorphosis" (11). Now the idea that form is rendered intelligible only to the extent that it is ceaselessly *deformed* is akin to the poststructuralist notion of the sign's regress. Like a divinity whose presence is sensed only through acts of disguise and disappearance, meaning in language is grasped only through the sign, which is nothing more than the mask of meaning's absence.

Similar to the intellectual *démarche* with which Rousseau opens his *Deuxième discours*, Calasso casts his mind back to an imaginary moment in order to explain our current inferior state. Rousseau's hypothetical historical moment provides a provocative explanation as to the nature of inequality among people. Calasso employs myth

---

[3] Naomi Wolf has coined the term "The Diana Principle" in order to conceptualize a new form of female empowerment based not on an awareness of victimization but rather on principles of retribution and action. See her book *Fire with Fire: The New Female Power and How it will Change the Twenty-first Century* (New York: Random House, 1993).

in order to portray the instant in which the Greek principle of metamorphosis was replaced by a fallen state in which forms became irrevocably fixed. This instant, he theorizes, was that of Persephone's abduction by Death:

> With the abduction of Persephone, death acquires a body, acquires body ... [i]n the past, few had had the privilege of being led by a god to the Elysian fields with their bodies still intact. And Hades was defined as that place where there is no body... But now ... [t]he world had reached a point at which the economy of metamorphosis that had sustained it for so long through the period of Zeus's adventures was no longer enough. Things had lost their primordial fluidity, had hardened into profile ... From now on, it was a question not only of accepting life in a single immutable form but of accepting the certainty that that form would one day disappear without trace [sic]. Demeter's anger is the revolt against this new regime of life. (211-12)

Calasso's hypothesis of the Greek fall from the plenitude of fluidity into limitation and immutability offers rich possibilities for feminist inquiry. First, it is through the possession of a mortal maiden that Death manifests itself and, achieving this, separates itself from the living realm. Here we see the twin operation of death and femininity as well as the original *putting down* of woman into the pit of unconscious non-existence. Assigned to darkness and silence, culture *named* Woman the uncanny boundary-line between life and death –she is not essentially so. Second, Calasso identifies Demeter's anger as a reaction of outrage to the newly divided realms.

Like Rousseau's second discourse, Calasso's imaginative theory points out the chasm between *now* and *then*: he distinguishes between the Greek principle of *Theós*–the "indeterminate divine" or "the perfection of the undifferentiated"–and Western principles of limitation and division (206-07). What I am proposing is that the claims of Deconstruction and Postmodernism might not be *new* at all but rather ancient. Postmodern inquiry may be said to cultivate an esthetic that is reminiscent of Antiquity, reveling in its own instability. It is within this ancient-postmodern theoretical framework that I turn now to an appreciation of Riccoboni's text *Lettres de Mistress Fanni Butlerd*.

MARIE-JEANNE RICCOBONI: *LE VÉCU ET L'ÉCRIT*

Marie-Jeanne Riccoboni published her first work of fiction in 1757 under the unwieldy title *Lettres de Mistress Fanni Butlerd à milord Charles Alfred de Caitombridge, comte de Plisinte, duc de Raslingth, écrites en 1735, traduites de l'anglois en 1756 par Adélaïde de Varençai*, choosing the mask of an invented name and presenting her original creation as an English translation. Thanks in part to the work of scholars such as Joan Stewart and Andrée Demay, Riccoboni's works have been re-printed and interest in her life and work has been resuscitated. The history of the text's publication sheds light on the socio-political situation of the eighteenth-century writer and is outlined fully by Joan Stewart in her introduction to the edition published in 1979 by Droz. Demay offers a short plot summary that I offer to readers not familiar with the work:

> Fanni, jeune fille mêlée à la haute société mais sans fortune, aime Sir Charles dont elle se croit aimée. Cédant à ses prières instantes, elle devient sa maîtresse alors que des devoirs militaires vont l'entraîner loin d'elle. A son retour, tandis qu'elle espère voir leur amour révélé et leur mariage fixé, il l'abandonne pour une union plus avantageuse à laquelle il se prétend contraint. Il lui offre cependant de poursuivre leur liaison secrète, acte de duplicité qu'elle repousse avec dégoût. (23)

Stewart affirms that "le roman est d'un rare dépouillement ... il n'y a quasiment pas ... d'intrigue ... c'est un roman sur rien" (xiv). The scarcity of action is incontestable; however, it must be noted that the attention paid by Riccoboni to psychological development rivals that of Rousseau, and may even have influenced the composition of *Julie*.[4] Concerning the question of biographical influences in Riccoboni's *oeuvre* generally, some scholars have advanced a certain conflation between *le vécu* and *l'écrit*. Interpretive statements based on biographical facts inform the criticism of Colette Piau–"[o]n évoque ici les *Lettres de Fanny Butlerd* donc le vécu" (379)–and Emily Crosby: "[o]n est anglaise, française, jeune fille, femme

---

[4] See page xxv of Joan Stewart's introduction to *Lettres de Mistress Fanni Butlerd* (1979) regarding the provocative possibility that Riccoboni may have influenced Rousseau's conception of his protagonist Julie.

mûre? N'importe, on est toujours Marie Jeanne Riccoboni" (83). Crosby limits the possibilities for reception further by placing all of Riccoboni's heroines into one of two categories: either they are shadows of the author herself or they are reflections of the author's dear friend Marie-Thérèse Biancolelli (83). Joan Stewart reconsiders this conflation of life with work by questioning it:

> The personal use [Riccoboni] made of her first novel, *Lettres de Mistress Fanni Butlerd* (1757), complicates the relation between invention and autobiography: the love letters of Fanni Butlerd to Alfred, the man who finally abandons her, may be read as models for the impassioned letters that Marie Jeanne Riccoboni later addressed over a period of more than seventeen years to Robert Liston. (*Gynographs* 72)

In a note that follows this paragraph, Stewart asserts that "Fanni's letters were themselves inspired by an unhappy love affair" (222) but later speaks insightfully of "complex mirroring" rather than utter transparency when considering the rapport between Riccoboni's life and work (*Gynographs* 74).

Informed by Philippe Lejeune's notion that even so-called official autobiography can never mirror lived experience, my approach to the text will be primarily esthetic rather than biographical or historical. I aim to demonstrate that Riccoboni's heroine writes in order to explore and express a longing that has as its source a double loss. Writing becomes a reconciliation of loss occasioned by a brother's death and a lover's indifference. By writing and publishing her correspondence and by manipulating her lover's portrait, Fanni expresses the full range of her desires through a kaleidoscopic system based on substitutions of presence. Her artistic mode of being, illustrative of the Greek concept of the "perfection of the undifferentiated," allows her to envision presence in Art where life hands her absence (Calasso 207). This mastery over words and the gaze proves to be subversive within the *petite communauté* to which she is consigned: it destabilizes the conventional subject-object opposition and brings about in its place a certain relational fluidity. I shall demonstrate that Fanni pays a high price for the growth made possible by artistic expression–that price is isolation and alienation, to which she responds privately through mournful suffering, and publicly, by publishing her correspondence.

FANNI THE WRITER

Numerous narrative and thematic elements–beginning with the first epistle, entitled "Miss Fanni à un seul lecteur"–lead me to dwell upon the fact that Fanni is first and foremost a writer. This initial letter encodes a paradox between private communication and public consumption, since intimate, if hateful, sentiments are being published for all to read. First, then, this initial utterance establishes that Fanni has published her correspondence. Such a paradox illustrates the uneasy collapse between personal and public experienced by the writer generally, the heart laid bare for the stranger's stare. I shall soon demonstrate how such instances of *collapse* within signifying oppositions such as public/private and subject/object drive Fanni's desire and Art. Second, it is evident that Fanni is very well-read: she refers to works by Alexander Pope, Mme de Lafayette, Diderot, Honoré d'Urfé, and Shakespeare; Joan Stewart has also pointed out the possibility of allusions to Marivaux and Crébillon fils.[5] In addition, Fanni alludes to the mythological figure of Iphis (Letter LVI) and to the Biblical figure of Solomon (Letter 42). Third, the reader learns in Letter 34 that this literary heroine is fluent in English, Spanish, and French (47).

In terms of the diegesis, then, it is clear that Fanni is a published writer and a well-read intellectual. To ignore the fact that Riccoboni's protagonist is a woman *writer* in love is to shortchange the potential of the text. As I shall illustrate through a discussion of the coveted portrait, Fanni's conflict is based not on simple oppositions between dream vs. reality or Ideal vs. real; there is a third term that the reader must consider, as she does, and that is her Art. Artistic creation allows her to sustain the illusion of presence while she sounds out the depths of her loss. Through acts of imagination

---

[5] For literary allusions in *Fanni Butlerd* see the following letters: Alexander Pope (Letters 26 and 50), Mme de Lafayette (Letter 39), Diderot (Letter 25), d'Urfé (Letter 74), and Shakespeare (Letter 89). Joan Stewart has additionally pointed out the possibility of allusions to Marivaux and Crébillon fils (*FB* 193-196). Here I would like to point out additional probable allusions to Corneille and Racine. In Letter 58 Fanni's "Tout me déplaît, m'ennuie et m'afflige" recalls Phèdre's "Tout m'afflige et me nuit, et conspire à me nuire" (Act I, scene iii). In Letter 109 her exclamation "Ah je ne vous hais point ..." is redolent of Chimène's famous *vers de douleur*.

and conjuration, she collapses distinctions between self and other, near and far. The question she asks in her first letter—*qu'a-t-on besoin de la réalité?*—shows her to be a true Romantic, interested less in life itself than in the possibility of its representation, which is to say its death.

Fanni draws upon the myth of Pygmalion in the opening portion of her correspondence in order to express the fall *out of* self-possessed indifference and *into* obsessed love:

> Semblable à Pigmalion, vous animez un marbre; craignez qu'il ne vous reproche un jour de l'avoir tiré de sa paisible insensibilité. (Letter 7, 11)

The metaphor of pale marble warming into blushing flesh expresses Fanni's transformation from an object of male contemplation to a speaking subject who foreshadows the demise of desire. The predominance of metaphor here underscores the text's content, which is love's illusion:

> Comment redouter un sentiment que vous peignez si pur, si désintéressé? Une ombre favorable fait sortir à nos yeux mille couleurs brillantes, et nous cache une partie du sujet varié qui s'offre à notre contemplation; cette ombre s'étend, le tableau magique se couvre de fleurs; pense-t-on en les voyant, aux épines dont la plus belle est environnée? ... Ah, laissez-moi; votre langage est si flatteur, vous parlez si bien!...... [sic] Je suis prête à douter..... [sic] Eh ne vous aimerais-je pas, si je vous croyais? (Letter 5, 9)

Through the use of multiple metaphors, the protagonist articulates a conception of love that is recognizably *dix-huitièmiste*: love is a paradox, a veil that both separates and unites, "une douce erreur" (Letter 1, 5). Love is a favorable shadow that spreads out to become a magic tableau of flowers with hidden thorns. Now while these metaphors may not seem particularly original, the layering or *rose-opening* of images attests to Riccoboni's originality. Throughout the text Fanni has recourse to this kind of rhetorical thicket of dense imagery, often inspired by or in response to other literary works.

Fanni's gift proves also to be a burden: increasingly, this writing woman finds herself at odds with the world of lived experience.

Letter 87 illustrates the extent to which her creative temperament isolates her from the realm of the quotidian. The letter, as always addressed to the absent Alfred, begins with an indication of physical location: "[j]e vous écris dans le cabinet de miss Betsi" (142). This private, enclosed space becomes the space of conjuration through remembrance:

> Je suis sur ce même sofa où vous faisiez si bien le malade pour être plaint, caressé, pour obtenir le pardon de toutes vos petites folies. Ah, quel jour! vous en souvient-il, mon cher Alfred? (142)

Now while she is alone and absorbed in inscribing *le souvenir*, real life is going on in the salon though she pays no heed:

> Grand dieu, quel bruit! quelle querelle! Sir Thomas est perdu! En prenant le thé, il vient de faire tomber une porcelaine admirable, elle est cassée. Si c'était le chat, miss en rirait; elle trouverait qu'il aurait eu de la grâce à faire cette sottise; mais sir Thomas est un 'mal-adroit' ... Pauvre sir Thomas! Il pleure, je crois; il contemple la belle tasse gisante sur le parquet ... Moi, j'écris toujours, je ne veux pas prendre parti, et je reste tranquille au milieu de l'orage. Le coeur me bat en songeant à demain.... (143-44)

In this anecdote I see the dilemma of the writer depicted in bold romantic strokes: the writer is removed from lived experience and truly lives only through artistic expression. The price of creation is the loss of participation in life.

This feeling of alterity is expressed in the letter in several ways. In space, Fanni's removal from the sphere of action is symbolic of the writer's distanced position as observer. In time, the act of writing robs the creator of the present moment: in *relating* present actions she is necessarily drawn away from them. The present moment offers nothing beyond a blank page upon which she inscribes remembrance of past pleasure and hope for future events: "je vous y ai vu, je vous y reverrai bientôt" (142). With respect both to space and time Fanni remains remote. Concerning action, as well, she makes her wish known: "j'écris, je ne veux pas prendre parti" (144). For this writer, the sphere of action is unpredictable and imperfect: teacups fall and break, people yell and cry. Writing provides a refuge from real events and creates a separate reality for her.

Desire and the Letter

In *Lettres de Mistress Fanni Butlerd* Riccoboni presents the relationship between loss and longing through the eyes and words of a woman writer. From the opening letter, love is described as an illusion that cannot be sustained–ultimately, "la réalité ... détruit le bonheur dont nous jouissons" (Letter 1, 5-6). Fanni never diverts her attention from the friction between love's illusion and life's reality. Early on in the correspondence, she demonstrates a keen prescience that the veil will one day fall: she records intimations of "la froideur succédant à la tendresse" (Letter 7, 11) and speaks of the time "[q]uand mon cher Alfred ne m'aimera plus" (Letter 51, 71). Later in the correspondence, she practically incites Alfred to infidelity when she writes "quand vous cesserez de m'aimer" (95, 153). As was the case with Graffigny's protagonist Zilia, Riccoboni's artist-heroine calculates love's losses with a mixture of Classical restraint and romantic fervor. While she cannot hold onto the beloved object in life, she can preserve and remember through artful gestures of representation. Ultimately, it is through representation that this young woman writer grieves and, through grieving, grows.

As is always the case in epistolary writing, the letter functions metonymically as a synecdoche of someone longed-for but gone. Riccoboni's exploration of the letter as shadow-presence differs little from that of her contemporaries (Graffigny, Marivaux) and her successors (Rousseau, Laclos); for this reason I shall not belabor it here. Suffice it to say that Fanni treats the letter as a fetish, stating simply in Letter 12 "[q]ue votre lettre est tendre! qu'elle est vive! qu'elle est jolie! je l'aime ... [j]e l'aime mieux que vous; je vous quitte pour la relire" (16). Elsewhere she writes of placing Alfred's cherished letters *au sein* and of bathing them with kisses and tears (Letters 48, 66 and 60, 85). This is all rather precious and tedious; however, beyond the basics of the diegesis one can ascertain an esthetic that I call "ancient-postmodern"–that is, one that simultaneously captures something of Greek sensibility and illustrates the postmodern concept of relational fluidity. As I have proposed, both the Greek ideal of metamorphosis and the feminist concept of polymorphism envision a freedom from the binary subject-object construction. As a vehicle of metonymy that operates on the basis of substitution, the letter mitigates the loss inscribed by physical absence and makes possible a kind of idealized presence. Fanni copes with Alfred's indifference and betrayal by replacing his physical person with a symbolic *continuum of presence*: "Alfred" becomes a *signifié* whose many *signifiants* include a scent (Letter 31, 42), a room, a painted gaze or trace of ink.

THE PORTRAIT: DESIRE AND THE GAZE

The role of the portrait in the *Lettres de Mistress Fanni Butlerd* is central to the text, yet it has not been adequately explored.[6] Approximately fifteen of the text's one hundred and sixteen letters contain descriptions or observations concerning the portrait of the absent lover. This visual representation of the beloved fulfills a crucial function within what I have called the symbolic continuum of presence. From an initial attitude of critical indifference, Fanni grows increasingly fond of Alfred's image and quickly begins to covet it as a *portrait-part* for the *whole*. Ultimately, the portrait becomes the primary element in a system of substitutions designed to compensate for an empty reality. The ersatz gaze provides a mute answer to the question "comment vous remplacer! quel amusement mettre à la place de ce plaisir vif qu'inspire la présence d'un homme que l'on adore?" (Letter 85, 139). The portrait as *copy* allows for a symbolic blending of the subject-object opposition; once again, representation satisfies more than lived experience.

In Joan DeJean's convincing study of *La Princesse de Clèves*, she refutes Luce Irigaray's interpretation of the gaze by asserting that "[t]he gaze has been forbidden to women, but that does not mean that they have not used it" ("Looking" 34). Irigaray posits that women have been victimized within a "dominant scopic economy"

---

[6] Jean Rousset provides a thoughtful analysis of the portrait in the eighth chapter of his book *Leurs yeux se rencontrèrent: la scène de première vue dans le roman*; however, he treats only those texts in which the encounter with the portrait *precedes* the actual meeting: Lafayette's *Zaïde*, Gomberville's *Polexandre*, Sorel's *Histoire comique de Francion*, and others. My approach looks at the encounter with the image as a shadow following physical presence: this is the function of the portrait in Lafayette's *La Princesse de Clèves*, Riccoboni's *Lettres de Mistress Fanni Butlerd*, and Rousseau's *Julie*. Within this framework the portrait serves to remind the subject of what was and is no more–it is memory rendered (and rent) in cloth and paint.

in which the female submits to being an object of contemplation by the male gaze (DeJean 34). Once again we see a line of feminist reasoning that upholds the very paradigm it seeks to deconstruct. By acknowledging that this paradigm is merely a construction, DeJean suggests, contemporary feminist critics can get beyond it:

> It may be that readers have not been sensitive to Woman's invasion of the 'dominant scopic economy' because the female erotic gaze does not function according to the model that male representations have schooled us to expect. ("Looking" 34)

By *unschooling* her own critical gaze DeJean successfully presents an example of a woman writer "[who] portray[s] a female desiring subject in the process of expressing her desire" (35). As a depiction of this process she examines the famous episode in *La Princesse de Clèves* in which the princess is seen (by Nemours and by the reader/spectator) in the act of weaving yellow and black ribbons around a cane. She then walks slowly over to the portrait of her forbidden love and gazes at it in rapt self-absorption. DeJean mentions the importance of the fact that the princess "stares not at the male object of her desire, but at his representation" (43). It is this relationship between the amorous female gaze and the portrait as copy or imitation that I undertake to develop in the context of Riccoboni's letter-text.

L'AIMABLE PORTRAIT: IDÉE ET OBJET

At first, the portrait is an *idea* in Fanni's imagination and not an object of contemplation in the physical world. In Letter 10 this *épistolière* conjures an image of her absent correspondent in her mind: "je vois l'aimable portrait se former sous mes yeux; il m'offre un tout.... Ah ce tout, est tout pour moi!" (14). In this exclamation I see the operation of metonymy: the portrait is a part used to signify the whole—*il m'offre un tout*. The entire letter constitutes an exploration of visual evocation: "quoiqu'un même objet semble fixer toutes mes idées, j'ai pourtant l'art de les étendre et de les varier" (14). It is noteworthy here that imagined presence has already begun to encroach upon actual presence, since the mental image offers internal riches unparallelled by any object in the external world.

From the imagined *idea* of a portrait Fanni next considers a *literary* portrait and holds her mental picture up to it; Riccoboni has yet to introduce the physical object. In Letter 39 the young writer recounts the activities of a quiet afternoon: lost in thought, she again removes herself from the sphere of experience:

> [Miss Betzi] a commencé à lire tout haut son maudit français, séparant chaque phrase, et mettant *Zaïde* en pièces: moi je n'écoutais point ... et je disais, *fort bien, à merveille, on ne peut mieux*. Cependant le portrait de Consalve a ramené mon attention; je me suis imaginé qu'il vous ressemblait; si beau, si bien fait, l'air noble, le coeur tendre, le naturel doux.... En vérité, il vous ressemble. (53)

In this letter Fanni speaks with (insincere) words but thinks in pictures. She takes pleasure in comparing her own mental image of Alfred to the literary depiction of Consalve, who is none other than the idealized *jeune homme* of Mme de Lafayette's 1671 *Histoire espagnole* entitled *Zaïde* (Stewart *FB* 195).[7] In her mind, Fanni compensates for Alfred's absence by casting him into the impossible, ideal realm of representation. Her substitution of Art for life has begun and relies upon a shaky equivalency between truth and resemblance: "[e]n vérité, il vous ressemble."

About a third of the way into the text (Letter 43) the reader suddenly learns that Fanni is in possession of an actual painted por-

---

[7] Lafayette's *Zaïde* may well have influenced the composition of Ricoboni's text. The portrait there plays a pivotal role and almost becomes a character in its own right, as Rousset implies:

> Le visage contemplé est absent: la vision et 'l'inclination' précèderont la rencontre, ou, si l'on préfère, celle-ci se répartit sur deux séquences séparées. Zaïde aperçoit dans un médaillon le portrait d'un jeune homme, elle est 'surprise de l'agrément decette peinture,' un astrologue lui déclare qu'elle est 'destinée' à cet inconnu; voilà l'une des fonctions du portrait, quand on ignore l'identité du modèle, ce qui est la règle: il combine l'énigme et la prophétie (*Leurs yeux* 150)

Ricoboni does not follow the chronological order described by Rousset. Her protagonist sees, knows, and loves the model–Alfred–*before* growing attached to his portrait; at least this is what the reader assumes given that there is no mention of the portrait as object before Letter 43. This chronology reverses the order in *Zaïde* in which the encounter with the portrait precedes physical contact. By reversing this order Ricoboni emphasizes regret and reflection over eager anticipation. Similar to Rousseau, she explores loss and longing as the fruits not only of physical separation but also of physical union. With Ricoboni and Rousseau the gaze is an Orphic, backward glance and not a forward-looking vision.

trait of her absent correspondent: "[l]e voilà, ce portrait, qu'il est différent de vous! Votre lettre ... m'offre ces traits chéris que je cherche vainement dans cette image...." (58). The circumstances concerning how and when she came to own it are not accessible to the reader–the portrait simply *appears*. I remain puzzled by this and can speculate only that Riccoboni is asking the reader to fill in a narrative gap without her assistance. Whatever its origin, this portrait comes to occupy a central role in Letters 43-85 and will *disappear* from the diegesis near the end of the correspondence, just prior to Fanni's discovery that Alfred has left her to marry a wealthy noblewoman. What then is the function of this enigmatic, ersatz gaze?

CE PORTRAIT ... ME DEVIENT CHER

Throughout the second third of this epistolary text, letters and pictures comprise a metonymic economy of desire in which partial representations stand in as substitutes for the plenitude of presence. This verbal-visual economy articulates a form of desire that is "strangely plural, capable of functioning in reality and in 'rêverie'" (DeJean 44). From an initial stance of critical indifference toward the painted vision of her *amant*, Fanni decides that this vision is pleasing ... so pleasing, in fact, that she brings it into her bed! But first things first. Before the picture becomes a fetish, she questions the value of the image as it relates to the written word and finds that Alfred's letters are a closer approximation of his being (Letter 43, 58). Gradually, however, she begins to favor the image as Alfred's military obligations take him further and further away from her and as he writes less and less often:

> Vous fuyez, mon cher Alfred; vous vous éloignez avec vitesse d'une femme qui vous adore: hélas où êtes-vous déjà? ce portrait est donc tout ce qui me reste? ... Il me paroît moins mal qu'hier; à force de le tourner, de le pencher, j'y trouve une ombre légère de ce que j'aime, je sens qu'il me devient cher ... En vérité, je l'aimerai, je l'aime déjà; l'habit me plaît: le premier jour où je vous l'ai vu, est bien présent à ma mémoire.... (Letter 44, 59)

Here DeJean's interpretation of the female gaze may be fruitfully applied, for this passage clearly illustrates that *represented presence* can be the occasion for rituals of remembrance. DeJean affirms that "[women writers] use the gaze to memorialize, to present a memory of passion that their heroines may prefer to the erotic present" (45). It is certain that in the passage quoted above, the picture allows Fanni to revisit past pleasures of which the present moment finds her bereft.

While Lafayette presents the desiring female subject tentatively, in deference to Classical dictates of understatement and restraint, Riccoboni's exploration is expansive and bold. Where Lafayette allows the reader to glimpse her protagonist's desire only momentarily, Riccoboni presents a succession of letters (43-85) in which Fanni is wholly inhabited by her passion. In continued contrast to her Classical predecessor, Riccoboni lays bare a vast vocabulary of the female gaze: Fanni not only looks at the portrait but also caresses it (146), punishes it (92), and ultimately speaks to it (138)! The reader witnesses Fanni's increasing fetishism concerning the painted *copy* of the beloved body: not limiting her thoughts to the past, she also inscribes the picture within an imagined future:

> [q]uand mon cher Alfred ne m'aimera plus ... je me ferai catholique ... [l]e portrait que je tiens de sa main, placé dans le lieu le plus éminent, sera le patron révéré ... couronné de fleurs, et couvert d'un voile léger, il ne sera vu que de moi.... (Letter 51, 71)

Alongside such fantasies of religious adoration the reader witnesses scenes where Fanni brings the portrait into her bed (pp. 62 and 100), places it in a dresser drawer to spend the night "en pénitence ... pour lui apprendre à me montrer de la joie quand je suis de mauvaise humeur" (72), and debates over where to hang it once it has been withdrawn from the dark drawer of penitence! (92). In a comical culmination of her fetishism, Fanni confides to Alfred–the copy's flesh-and-blood original–that she beats the picture:

> Votre portrait en pâtit, je m'en prens à lui, il est mis en pénitence au fond, tout au fond du tiroir. On vous dira comme je le bats, comme il est malheureux avec moi.... (Letter 72, 108)

Un cher portrait indeed! How might one best regard these exhibitions? To say that these are merely vain ravings of an irrational woman would be inaccurate and the easy way out, for Riccoboni consistently balances feeling with thinking, fantasy with philosophy.[8] To understand this section of the correspondence I believe it is necessary truly to *look at* this portrayal of a woman's desire straight on, without blinking, in the (lost) tradition of the goddess Artemis. If such an unabashed stance is difficult to adopt, Joan DeJean tells us, it is because "we are accustomed to deciphering only the male gaze" (45).

The limpid gaze of the virgin huntress Artemis is the lens through which we can apprehend Riccoboni's *mise en scène* of the scopic economy. I am suggesting that this economy operates metonymically through shifting, successive representations. Through artful substitutions of the part for the whole and imaginative acts of conjuration, Riccoboni depicts that aspect of desire that is predicated upon loss. In *Fanni Butlerd,* the female gaze speaks in a language that diffuses a unified concept of the subject-object distinction, since it enjoys the more lasting *substitutions* of presence–writing and the portrait–over and above the fleeting reality of physical union.

Melancholy and Metonymy

In *Gender Trouble* Butler reassesses Freud's essay "Mourning and Melancholia" (1917) from a feminist perspective; I shall make reference to her contribution here as I consider Fanni's double process of writing and mourning.[9] According to Butler, who is re-stating Freud, melancholy may be defined as an "internalizing strategy" that allows the ego to survive the loss of a love-object precisely by incorporating aspects of that same object within its very structure

---

[8] Letters 14, 15, 16 and 114 contain particularly interesting philosophical passages.

[9] Butler accepts Freud's interpretation of melancholy for the most part, but states that "there has been little effort to understand the melancholic denial/preservation of homosexuality in the production of gender within the heterosexual frame" (57). Her recapitulation of Freud's essay accounts for the double loss incurred by the female infant, who must first renounce her primary homosexual cathexis (the mother) and then relinquish the first heterosexual love object (the father). The female subject therefore moves through two taboos while the male subject confronts only one.

(58). The loss of the object may be attributed to "separation, death, or the breaking of an emotional tie" (64). Butler explains that melancholic incorporation belies a certain refusal of loss and also relies upon incantation and ritualization:

> In the experience of losing another human being whom one has loved ... the ego is said to incorporate that other ... taking on attributes of the other and sustaining the other through magical acts of imitation ... [t]he melancholic refuses the loss of the object, and internalization becomes a strategy of magically resuscitating the lost object, not only because the loss is painful, but because the ambivalence felt toward the object requires that the object be retained until differences can be settled. (57, 61-62)

Here she speaks of melancholy as a somber memorial in which the gaze of the one who has gone glows dimly and inwardly in the mind of the one who remains. The paradox is that the melancholic preserves the loss, keeping it present and accessible until such time that it may finally be faced and released.

Let us look at two scenes of melancholy in Riccoboni's text in order to ascertain more closely the function of Fanni's metonymic scopic economy. The first scene (Letter 78) occurs about two-thirds of the way through the correspondence and follows a brief but significant passage in the preceding letter. In Letter 77 the reader learns of a momentous loss in Fanni's life–the death of her brother:

> Quand je pleurois mon frère, mylord Stanley me repétoit sans cesse que j'étais foible. Si donner des pleurs à la perte de ce qu'on aimoit, est la marque d'une âme foible, la mienne est foible, et le sera toujours. (120)

Behind the stubborn absence of the *amant*, then, there is a more absolute loss inscribed by the separation of death. The double blow of the brother's death and the lover's absence therefore presents itself as the *wound-source* of mourning that Fanni will ultimately name *la mélancolie* (155).

The letter following the mention of the brother's death may be read as a *mise en scène* of melancholy in that the pleasures of *substituted* presence allow the subject to mourn her loss. In Letter 78

Fanni recounts to Alfred how she spent a solitary afternoon engaged in phantom communication with various representations of him:

> Je me suis levée bien matin aujourd'hui, pour jouir de ma liberté. Tout le monde était allé à Canterbury. Quel plaisir de me trouver seule! vous auriez ri de me voir. C'est pour le coup que miss Betzi pouvoit dire que j'avois l'air d'une princesse de roman. Votre portrait sur ma table, vos lettres éparses dans mon sein, sur mes genoux; le tiroir renversé, le porte-feuille ouvert, je contemplais mes richesses. (120-21)

It is evident here that Riccoboni invites–or forces–her reader to adopt a stance of voyeurism in order to depict this grieving, desiring female subject. In a probable allusion to the Princesse de Clèves, Riccoboni calls her protagonist a *princesse de roman* and surrounds her with symbolic stand-ins for the lost lover. These substitutions *approximate* presence and compensate the loss: the painted gaze and the written word become idealized evocations inscribed within Fanni's own conception of self.[10] The sustaining gesture through substitution is at the heart of the melancholic's strategy. It is, moreover, not unlike the sustaining gesture of language itself, in which the sign stands in as a constant reminder of what is not there.

---

[10] How different is Rousseau's incorporation of the portrait! In *La Nouvelle Héloïse*, Julie sends her portrait to Saint-Preux whom Claire has banished from the *petite communauté*. In Book II, Letter 22, Saint-Preux records his reactions to the picture and his reception of it:
> Je tenais donc ce paquet avec une inquiète curiosité dont je n'étais pas le maître; je m'efforçais de palper à travers les enveloppes ce qu'il pouvait contenir ... j'ai senti palpiter mon coeur à chaque papier que j'ôtais, et je me suis bientôt trouvé tellement oppressé que j'ai été forcé de respirer un moment sur la dernière enveloppe ... Julie! ... ô ma Julie! le voile est déchiré ... je te vois ... Dieux! quels tourments de flammes mes avides regards puisent dans cet objet inattendu! ô comme il ranime au fond de mon coeur tous les mouvements impétueux que ta présence y faisait naître!" (200-01)

Here the (male) gaze is subordinated to tactile experience and the act of seeing is described as an act of aggression: "mes regards puisent dans cet objet." While Rousseau treats the portrait primarily as an object to be handled and possessed, Riccoboni makes of the portrait a window through which the (female) gaze might view the past anew.

Riccoboni presents her second scene of melancholy in Letter 85; like the scene I have just examined, this one is distinct in that Fanni occupies herself with both visual and verbal substitutes for the lost beloved(s). Through the double incorporation of word and gaze she establishes a system of substitutions designed to keep the loss close:

> Vous voilà debout sur ma table, appuyé contre mon écritoire, votre lettre sert de piédestal à la jolie statue: ses yeux fixés sur les miens semblent vouloir faire passer dans mon coeur le feu dont ils brillent: cette bouche qui sourit, paroît vouloir s'ouvrir pour me parler. (137-38)

Here, as in Letter 78, the mourning-desiring Fanni resuscitates the lost object through acts of imitation (Butler 57, 61). As long as she seeks to create this kind of uncanny presence she refuses the loss and feeds the wound. Butler points out that this strategy of conjuration continues until that point in time when the subject can give up the lost object and surrender the substitutes once and for all. This Fanni achieves in the final portion of her correspondence: her mournful introversion is transformed into anger, and her private correspondence is printed for public consumption.

If there is any doubt as to whether Riccoboni encodes melancholy within her exploration of female desire, it is erased in Letters 96 and 97. In them her protagonist writes "ce trouble dont je ne puis me défendre, est une maladie de mon âme ... c'est l'effet d'une imagination trop remplie d'un seul objet ... l'amour, quand il est extrême, porte naturellement à la mélancolie" (154-55). When imagination finds itself confronted with loss or impossibility, there will be melancholy; for the artist, the process of grieving can be the occasion for artistic creation, releasing him or her back to health. This is the path that I assign to Fanni, who works through her bereavement to achieve a certain wisdom about herself: "mon coeur, trompé par ses désirs, éclairé par ses peines, n'a joui que d'une vaine erreur. Il la regrette peut-être, mais il ne peut la recouvrer" (191). Ultimately, Riccoboni has her heroine choose life over representation–life with all its imperfection, broken teacups, promises, and noise. This lucid embrace with reality, however, punctuates the end of a psychological exploration that is romantic in nature. The romantic esthetic does not belong to the nineteenth century nor to any other but is already flourishing at the heart of the Enlightenment and in the mind of Marie Jeanne Riccoboni who asks, in 1757, "qu'a-t-on besoin de la réalité?"[11]

---

[11] Andrée Demay also has made a convincing claim for Riccoboni's Romanticism:

> Fanni, qui reconnaît la force de ses désirs, éprouve la nécessité de les expliquer, et de donner l'excuse romantique ... [a]vant Rousseau et les poètes romantiques, Marie-Jeanne a souvent mis l'accent sur la force du souvenir, des lieux, des heures, des saisons. Mais si le coeur souffre, la détermination demeure inébranlable. (36-37)

V

DIVERSIONS OF DESIRE:
LETTRES DE MILADY JULIETTE CATESBY À MILADY HENRIETTE CAMPLEY, SON AMIE

Throughout this inquiry into the nature of the Lyric in epistolary texts of the Enlightenment, I have emphasized the notions of errancy, generic mixing, and the mask and have used myth and image to illustrate their meaning. With regard to genre, I have considered the epistolary text as a *carrefour* among theatrical, meditative, and narrative codes. In addition, I have demonstrated how letter-texts may be read as a kind of *poésie masquée*, subverting the sign through the incorporation of blank space and evocations of non-verbal codes. In the present discussion I shall focus on the ways in which these same notions reflect the esthetic that shaped the early period of the Enlightenment: the rococo. My analysis will proceed from a discussion of definition and historical situation to a close reading of Marie-Jeanne Riccoboni's text, *Lettres de Milady Juliette Catesby à Milady Henriette Campley, son amie* (1759). My premise is that this text bears the imprint of rococo structures with respect both to *forme* and to *fond*.

FROM ONE TO MANY: BAROQUE AND ROCOCO

The term *rococo* may be said to designate the eighteenth-century expression of Romanticism in literature and art. The rococo esthetic is generally thought to have developed as a refusal of Classicism and a refinement of the baroque; its evolution and demise are closely tied up with the socio-political circumstances of the early years of the eighteenth century. It effected a rupture with the grand style of Louis XIV in that it replaced heavy and grandiose architecture and decoration with a light, intricate style more suited to the interiors of the elegant *hôtels* in which noble men and women resided following the Regent's move from Versailles to Paris. This move from the Court to the city effected a symbolic shift from the public sphere to the private one; this displacement from *l'extérieur* to *l'intérieur* is thought to have provoked a new interest in the inner life of human minds and hearts.

H.W. Janson defines the rococo as an "intimate, flexible style [designed to] give greater scope to individual fancy uninhibited by classicist dogma" (556). He further points out that the word rococo

> was coined as a caricature of *rocaille* (echoing the Italian *barocco*), which meant the playful decoration of grottoes with irregular shells and stones. Rococo was a refinement in miniature of the curvilinear, "elastic" Baroque of Borromini and Guarini, and thus could be happily united with Austrian and German Late Baroque architecture. (556)

In the context of architecture and the visual arts, common characteristics of the rococo include a sense of movement, grace, light-heartedness, frivolity, playfulness, and an emphasis on color over line. In painting, the sensuous use of color marked the triumph of *Rubénisme* over *Poussinisme* (Levey 18). Throughout the present discussion I shall demonstrate how these characteristics may be found to operate in epistolary writing.

It is perhaps easier to see how the rococo effected a break with the Classical esthetic than to understand how it extended the baroque, for difference is sometimes apprehended more easily than resemblance. The contrast between the overbearing architecture of Versailles and the delicate interior of the *hôtel particulier*, for instance, is easily grasped, as is the contrast between canvases painted by Poussin and by Fragonard. To *compare* the baroque with the rococo, however, is a more subtle task and therefore a more difficult one. Janson bases his comparison on the notion of magnitude, calling the rococo a "refinement in miniature" of the baroque (556). The phenomenon of *petitesse* emerges as a primary characteristic of the rococo esthetic, as Carol Sherman explains in her article "Diderot et la rhétorique du rococo":

> Le rococo, à l'inverse du baroque, fait régner le petit. Peintures, intérieurs, et nouvelles constructions, tout est réduit par rapport

> au passé ... [s]alons et pavillons offrent alors un milieu parfait pour accueillir des objets menus—tabatières, boîtes à mouches—disposés sur de minuscules tables à écrire. (252)

Expanding the work of Philippe Minguet, Sherman calls this emphasis on smallness *emboîtement*, or miniaturization, and makes of it the first of five formal principles constituting the literary rhetoric of rococo: the remaining four she calls *l'enchevêtrement* (entanglement), *l'atectonicité* (asymmetry), *le jeu*, and *le rêve* (254-255). I shall refer to these valuable principles in my analysis of *Lettres de Milady Juliette Catesby*.

The rococo emphasis on *petitesse* has led art historians and literary critics to qualify this style as a refinement of the baroque. Unfortunately, critics since the time of Diderot have too often equated smallness with meaninglessness, frivolity with inanity. Art on a small scale did not seduce for very long, as Michael Fried points out:

> the primacy of absorption in French painting and criticism of the early and mid-1750s must be seen in connection with the reaction against the Rococo that began several years before (1747 is the date usually given). The basic features of this reaction [include] a turning away from the exquisite, sensuous, intimately decorative painting ... and an insistence on the need to return to what were perceived as the high seriousness, elevated morality, and timeless esthetic principles of the great art of the past.... (35)

Le petit, then, was to enjoy favor only for a while, perhaps for the duration of the childhood of Louis XV. As the new monarch grew, so did the size of canvases and novels: Watteau's small paintings and the short epistolary text gradually gave way to the expansive works of Jean-Louis David and Jean-Jacques Rousseau.

The contrast in magnitude offers a cogent illustration of the difference between baroque and rococo; however, the reduction in size has unfortunately been equated with a reduction in worth. One way around such an erroneous equivalency is to re-consider the literal definitions of the two terms. The term *baroque* is thought to have evolved from the Portugese *barroco* meaning a pearl of irregular shape, whereas the term *rococo* is defined as an ornamental grouping of stones and shells (Schneider 55). At the literal level, then, the baroque is one (one pearl) and the rococo is many (many shells or stones). In my view, the change from one to many manifests itself in the Art, philosophy, and literature of the period and reflects a new emphasis on society, or *communitas*.

Enlightenment artists and thinkers consistently entertained the question of the individual's role within society. Like the artful patterns of leaves, shells, or sinuous lines that decorated their furniture and walls, painters and writers peopled their canvases and manuscripts with groups in addition to individuals. Watteau's ensemble paintings of idle lovers, for instance, which were given the name of *fêtes galantes* by the Academy in 1717 (Levey 58), idealize the concept of community. How different is his canvas entitled "Gilles," in which the solitary Pierrot dressed in pearly white stands in awkward stasis, his back turned to the earthbound crowd at his feet! The graceful anguish of his gaze speaks of the isolation of the individual who stands apart from society. In literature, the importance of community is consistently upheld as well: Diderot regularly advocates the importance society–stating, for example, in *La Religieuse* that "l'homme est né pour la société" (153)–and Rousseau created in his Art the benevolent *petite communauté* that eluded him in life. I shall soon demonstrate how the idea of community operates in Riccoboni's text as well. The rococo esthetic, with its emphasis on ordered profusion, seems to reflect a new philanthropy: where the baroque is one, the rococo is many.

Theatricality and the Rococo Esthetic: Decoration and Décor

Rococo art is a theatrical one, and the theater (specifically, the *commedia dell'arte*) quickly became a beloved subject matter for rococo artists. Theatricality may therefore be said to operate as the third term of the syllogism I have just set forth, informing the rococo esthetic both in *forme* and in *fond*. With regard to form, the rococo developed primarily as an architectural and decorative art based on the embellishment of private space. Because of the spatial contingencies of the *hôtels particuliers*, wealthy Parisians transformed their living quarters into sumptuous, music-box spaces. Decorative designs covered walls and chairs and surfaces glittered with delicate *objets d'art*. This decorative mode cultivates illusion and therefore may be said to be governed by theatrical purpose. Carol Sherman observes that the *trompe l'oeil* effect of the rococo is related to the predominance of generic mixing in that art:

l'on joint volontiers et en trompe-l'oeil la peinture et l'architecture: souvent la dernière arche d'une série montante ou descendante est peinte et non construite. ("Diderot" 253)

Enclosed in such richly decorated private spaces, artists and philosophers gathered to discuss politics and recite essays and poems; there is a clear affinity between rococo decoration and theatrical décor.

If the rococo aspired toward a certain dramatization of life, it also took up the world of the theater for its subject matter. The architectural rococo transformed living spaces into veritable *mises-en-scène*, while the movement in painting and literature found in the world of the stage an ideal, social art form. Here it is important to point out that the theater memorialized and depicted was not that of the French tradition, but rather that of the *commedia dell'arte*. The presence of the *commedia* in Paris at this time was not devoid of meaning; it was a sign of change as well as a testament to artistic tolerance. The Italian players had entertained Louis XIV at Versailles and he had delighted in their fanciful antics and improvised dialogue; however, Mme de Maintenon banished them from the King's Court in 1697, objecting that they were coarse and salacious (Schneider 36). In 1716, at the invitation of the duc d'Orléans, the Italian comedians returned to France; this time they played not at Versailles but in the theaters of Paris.

This spatial shift from the Court to the city was a symbolic one. France's ruler–and with it France's art–had moved to the city to dwell among the people. The French, moreover, were now embracing a foreign tradition; and the Italian theater bore no resemblance to the Classical canon formed during the reign of the Sun King. The Italian comedians seduced noble and humble spectators alike with their *lazzi* (improvisational acrobatic movements), their *zanni* (character-types), and above all their *canevas* (recognizable plots). The *commedia* defied the Classical doctrine: instead of the immobile, upright presence of actors and actresses on a royal stage, the Italian comedians tumbled, ran, and danced in the streets. The *commedia* was of course not the only form of theater to be found in Paris during this period: Voltaire's plays continued to show deference to Classical dictates and if Marivaux's emphasis on psychological action and use of prose were new, he still honored the three unities. Nevertheless, the Italian players articulated–through words and gestures—a new esthetic that was soon to captivate artists working in almost every medium.

The Italian theater afforded the public of the early Enlightenment an escape from the Classical dramatic tradition. Perhaps more than any other art form, the *commedia* expressed the spirit of rococo art, here described by Michael Levey:

> The whole duty of the rococo was to release art from being the carrier of preconceptions; it need not contain a religious message, nor a moral one, and ultimately need not be serious at all. (35)

Critics since Diderot have attacked the rococo movement on the grounds of content, equating a lack of seriousness with a lack of purpose. The search for pleasure and the freedom to dream that characterize rococo painting and writing have been dismissed as vain and as feminine.[1] Yet despite such widespread underestimation, certain scholars have persisted in revealing the profundity masked by revelry: Michael Levey insists that in the pictorial rococo, "graceful form is complemented by serious content" (52) and Carol Sherman explains that "[l]'élégance et la grâce de la surface cachent un message dont le laconisme s'explique par l'habitude d'éviter les foudres de la censure ... [le rococo met en scène un] art qui montre sans dire et communique de l'intérieur" (260, 259).

Marie-Jeanne Riccoboni, *comédienne et épistolière*

Born one year before the death of Louis XIV, Marie-Jeanne Laboras de Mézières was a child of the Regency and was personally affected by its pleasures and failures. The disastrous outcome of Treasurer John Law's financial dealings in 1720 left her parents penniless, and after their deaths the young Marie-Jeanne found it necessary to earn a living (Crosby 12-13). Because she had been for-

---

[1] Michael Fried writes that the anti-rococo movement in France, which began mid-way through the eighteenth century, developed as a "deliberate attempt to recreate the grandeur of the reign of Louis XIV" (71). The rococo emphasis on visual abundance and fantasy was seen as "emasculating" and was replaced by a Neoclassical economy of color and line as evidenced in the canvases of Jean-Louis David.

tunate enough to receive a proper education, she was able to work by her wits instead of by her hands. She found work as an actress with the *Comédie Italienne* in 1734 and married one of its principal actors, François Riccoboni, in 1735 (Crosby 13). While she acted, she also wrote. In 1757, she published her *Lettres de Mistress Fanni Butlerd*: the text was widely popular, quickly sold out, and soon gave rise to numerous *contrefaçons* (Crosby 37, 45). In 1759, and now averaging one book per year, Marie-Jeanne Riccoboni published *Lettres de Milady Juliette Catesby à Milady Henriette Campley, son amie, par Marie de ****. Like *Fanni Butlerd* (1757) and *L'Histoire du Marquis de Cressy* (1758), *Juliette Catesby* was received with admiration: "critiques et public s'unirent pour les louer" (Crosby 37). Eighteenth-century readers grew curious about the identity of Juliette's creator; Riccoboni's friend Thérèse Biancolleli revealed her to be the long-time actress with the *commedia dell'arte* (Crosby 38). In 1759, Marie-Jeanne Riccoboni was forty-five years old and had been performing with the *commedia* for twenty-five years.

Juliette Catesby is a monophonic epistolary text told from the point of view of Juliette, a young English widow of high birth. For readers not familiar with the work I quote Joan Stewart's résumé of the plot, such as it is:

> [The text presents] Lady Juliette Catesby's account in letters to a confidante [Henriette Campley] of her relations with Milord d'Ossery. Engaged to the young widow Juliette, d'Ossery unaccountably abandons her for Jenny Montford. Upon Jenny's death about a year later, he again pursues a now perplexed and disgruntled Juliette. Eventually, he writes her a long letter explaining why he had suddenly transferred his suit to the less comely Jenny: having drunk too much during dinner at the home of Jenny's brother, he seduced her, and when she became pregnant, he married her. She gave birth and, forlorn, died of consumption a few months later. Now a widower, d'Ossery repents his errors; Juliette relents, and the two wed–a happy second marriage for each. ("Sex, Text" 60)

As is most often the case in epistolary writing, the ultimate *event* is *l'écriture*. Narrativity takes on a secondary importance while the charting of the psychological voyage emerges as the primary concern. Not only does the letter record the states of mind and heart, but the gesture of writing itself stimulates psychological change. In epistolary writing, what happens differs from what the text is *about*: in my view, this text is about how desire and individual honor (or virtue) operate to change a specific community. Stated another way, *Juliette Catesby* recapitulates the Cornelian dilemma in Enlightenment terms and from a feminist perspective.

In *Le Cid*, external actions within the larger community prevent Rodrigue and Chimène from being united. The first of these actions is the famous slap delivered by Le Comte Don Gomès to Don Diègue. Rodrigue avenges his father in the name of *gloire*, by which is meant honor in the eyes of the community. Further military actions in the name of the State ultimately prove the young lovers' allegiance to the King, who then declares that marriage is allowed since duty has been fulfilled. Within this economy of love and power, Chimène circulates as an object of political exchange, unable to act or even object: "[e]t quand un roi commande, on doit lui obéir" (V, vii, line 1804). Both personal honor and personal desire are effaced before the authority of King and State, and the collective good is valued above individual experience.

Juliette Catesby is also about love and duty, but here duty is a question of fidelity to one's self rather than to one's ruler. Individual honor–or virtue–enters into conflict with desire. In this text, there is no ruling seat of authority within this community of young, English idlers. Ensconced within the English countryside and preoccupied by social engagements rather than military ones, the Lords and Ladies form an ensemble and recall in literature the pictorial settings of Watteau's *fêtes galantes*. Like the figures in Watteau, Juliette and her friends and suitors are largely "engaged in the difficult business of doing nothing" (Schneider 54): they write letters, call on each other, stroll in parks and gardens, play music and dance. Life itself becomes a theatrical affair and plays itself out within the decorative rooms and manicured grounds of various English manors. Unlike Watteau's characters, whose eloquence is their silence, Riccoboni's *speak*. What they say reveals that while they may appear to "do nothing" they are in fact doing something: they are thinking and writing.

The community in *Juliette Catesby* reflects the socio-political world of the Regency: clearly stated, there is no centralization of authority. This lack of a central authority manifests itself within the diegesis. In terms of intrigue, there is no ruling voice: Juliette is perhaps the most important writer but she does not shape the correspondence alone. Henriette, her dearest friend, remains at a distance but her letters (of which the reader remains deprived) clearly affect Juliette's actions and thoughts. In Letter VI, for example, Henriette urges her *triste amie* to forgive Milord d'Ossery's betrayal: her letter requires Juliette to take a firm psychological stance and to reply "[v]ous me dites de pardonner à Milord d'Ossery, ou de ne plus penser à lui? Lui pardonner! Ah jamais!" (20). Milord d'Ossery is equally a strong voice in the correspondence, and his final letter with its interpolated story serves as a kind of *coup de théâtre*, as I shall later demonstrate. Together, Juliette, Henriette, and Milord d'Ossery alternatively serve to shape the narrative; as a result, there is not one but many centers of narrative authority, reflecting the esthetic shift from baroque to rococo.

The narrative world of *Juliette Catesby* is one in which no single character rules: just as there is no longer an absolute monarch in the political system, there is no longer a univocal narrator in the signifying system of this text. Riccoboni portrays the Cornelian dilemma and redefines the notion of *gloire* in Enlightenment terms: whereas *gloire* in Corneille is an affirmation of personal worth in the eyes of the State, it becomes in the eighteenth century a measure of personal integrity in one's own eyes. Juliette has been wronged by the man she desires and must decide for *herself* whether or not to forgive this wrong. Her entire correspondence records her anger, her indecision, and ultimately the desire that persists and allows her to forgive. An enlightened Chimène, she answers not to any King but to a more unknowable, internal ruler: herself. Like Marivaux's Silvia, she must look within and measure individual honor and desire on her own terms. In continued contrast to Corneille's baroque play, the beneficiary of Juliette's actions proves again to be herself and not the State.

Let us look at Juliette's dilemma more closely in order to ascertain the extent to which it reflects Enlightenment philosophy and the rococo esthetic. Like her fictional ancestral sisters, Juliette is caught in the impasse of desire; unlike them, the obstacle that keeps her from the object of her desire is internal and not external. For Chimène, the external obstacle is her father's honor–she cannot love the man who disgraced and killed her father until he absolves himself of his affront. For La Princesse de Clèves, the husband becomes an external obstacle that prevents her from loving the duc de Nemours. Although M. de Clèves finally dies from chagrin, his memory continues to obstruct the princess's thoughts and deeds. In contrast, Juliette is a widow unencumbered by past or present rulers; there is no mention of her parents or any other governing *body*–whether political or physical–in her life.

Juliette is relatively free compared to many of her fictional sisters. Nevertheless, she expresses a nuanced version of the Cornelian dilemma: the dilemma between love of another and duty to herself. Her fiancé Milord d'Ossery betrays her in order to fulfill his duty to Jenny Montfort; after Jenny conveniently dies, he asks again for Juliette's hand in marriage. Although she still desires him, she hesitates before a self-imposed obstacle of personal decorum: "[q]uelle dure bienséance me retient" (Letter 29, 120). In this letter, decorum is presented in terms of individual integrity rather than as an external measure of personal worth:

> ... Aimable et cher d'Ossery, tu m'accuses de cruauté! Que ne peux-tu lire dans mon coeur, entendre les voeux qu'il forme pour toi! Quelle dure bienséance me retient? Que ne m'est-il permis de voler auprès de toi! d'aller soulager, partager, adoucir tes maux ... Ah, ranime tes espérances! celle que tu chéris n'est point *cruelle*, n'est point *inhumaine*; elle peut te pardonner, te revoir, t'aimer! (Letter 29, 120)

This letter marks a definitive change in the diegesis since it shows Juliette on the brink of forgiving the repentant d'Ossery, an act that she had flatly refused in Letter 6. D'Ossery has not yet lived up to the standard that she has set; in order to remove her inner obstacle d'Ossery must show her a certain transparency by justifying his infidelity. This he achieves in a ruse that exemplifies the latent theatricality in much eighteenth-century literature: he speaks the truth from behind a mask.

The mask that d'Ossery dons is first literal and then symbolic. Approximately three-quarters of the way into the correspondence, Juliette relates to her friend Henriette that her wealth–normally of no interest to her–has allowed her to help her gardener Sara. The grandfather of Sara's intended, Tommy, has demanded that Sara's dowry be supplemented to equal the amount of Tommy's recent inheritance:

> Entre le bonheur et le malheur de ces simples et tendres amants, cent cinquante guinées s'élevaient comme une barrière insur-

> montable ... [c]e moment est un de ceux où j'ai senti l'avantage d'être riche. Je marie après demain mon aimable villageoise et je la marie avec éclat. Je donne un grand souper, illumination, feu et musique sur l'eau; ensuite un bal masqué où tout le monde sera le bien venu. (Letter 32, 128)

In Juliette's gesture one may glimpse the kind of ideal *fête* that Rousseau will soon create in *La Nouvelle Héloïse*, a community in which social class and economic difference are erased and where work and pleasure combine in perfect harmony. Unlike Clarens, however, Riccoboni allows for no governing voice or *oeil vivant* in the world she creates. Whereas the apparent harmony at Clarens is in fact the product of Wolmar's constant manipulation and control, the world painted by Riccoboni emerges as a true *locus amoenus*.

Into this *locus* d'Ossery comes, wearing the mask that he hopes will allow him to reveal the truth of his honorable conduct. After the masked ball, Juliette relates to Henriette (whose inability to attend makes possible the epistolary account) how d'Ossery surprised her by appearing there in disguise:

> Oh, ma chère Henriette ... quel trouble dans mon âme! ... je l'ai vu... il m'a parlé ... c'était lui ... il était au bal... Le jour était déjà grand; fatiguée de danser, ennuyée du bal, j'ai passé sur la terrasse pour prendre l'air. Un masque en domino noir, qui me suivait depuis une heure, est venu se placer à mes côtés. Dans un lieu aussi spacieux, j'ai trouvé un peu extraordinaire qu'on choisît l'endroit où j'étais pour m'y gêner; car le masque s'est assis tout près de moi. Mais jugez de ma surprise, quand saisissant une de mes mains, la retenant malgré moi ... ce masque m'a dit d'un ton ému: *Eh quoi, Lady Juliette se plaît encore de faire des heureux!* ... Je l'ai reconnu.... J'ai voulu fuir; l'audacieux s'est saisi de ma robe et m'a retenue dans ma place. Il a ôté brusquement son masque; son camail s'est renversé ... Ah, ma chère Henriette, qu'il était bien! Le désordre de ses cheveux donnait une grâce nouvelle à ses traits; un air animé, passionné même.... (Letter 34, 135-36)

Shaken by this dark form of recognition, and like any good *héroïne sensible*, Juliette swoons. When she regains consciousness, she is surrounded by "une infinité de personnes"; she scans the crowd for d'Ossery and finally spies him stealing away from the party–"il a disparu" (136).

D'Ossery fails in his attempt to reveal his truth from behind a mask. Undaunted, he puts on a new mask–that of writing. In the letter that follows Juliette's description of the masked ball, the reader learns that her anguished swoon was the result not of fear or hatred, but of ardent longing: "[o]n dit, ma chère, que l'absence est un remède salutaire contre l'amour; remède violent, que le malade prend toujours avec dégoût et qui n'opère pas sur tous les tempéraments" (Letter 35, 137-38). As she is absorbed in writing and brooding, her servant brings her "tout un cahier écrit de la main de Milord" (138). What follows is a letter in which is embedded the *histoire intercalée* of d'Ossery's exploits and amends. This time, the mask works: after a letter of reaction in which Juliette prepares to forgive, the reader learns in Letter 37 that "tout est pardonné, tout est oublié!" Like the characters in Marivaux's *Le Jeu de l'amour et du hasard*, Juliette and d'Ossery arrive at their truth–mutual desire–through sophisticated acts of masking. Dissimulation operates paradoxically as a means to an end–the transparency of revelation. Juliette wears a mask of impassibility in order to cover her vulnerability, and d'Ossery masks his sexual adventure behind a story of repentance that Juliette takes to be true.

The rococo esthetic informs this epistolary narrative and the ways in which this narrative is told. The rococo elements that I have discussed are the wandering narrative focal point, the character ensembles (reminiscent of Watteau's *fêtes galantes*), the decorative physical settings, and the symbolic masks that function as a kind of *trompe-le-coeur*. By adapting her subject matter from the French tradition and combining it with elements of the Italian comedies that she knew so well, Riccoboni stages a kind of *tableau parlant* in which the limits of honor and desire are first set and then tested in a world of recreation–conversation, correspondence, music, and masks. These *serious games* in which the characters engage bring about a psychological *recreation–à travers le jeu, le je s'interroge*.

LE (JE)U THÉÂTRAL DE L'ÉCRITURE ÉPISTOLIÈRE

In the theater the rococo artist discovered a form of communication that sought to express human experience through an esthetic based on diversion and illusion. Michael Levey points out that "[t]he rococo ... [cultivated] the artificial and unnatural. It was not true; but then art that was true was not always adequate, for it might be undignified or might fail to contain the higher truth of morality" (9). Here is stated in the language of the art historian the dilemma of eighteenth-century literature defined by Georges May: [f]allait-il ... embellir la nature humaine ... ou fallait-il, au contraire représenter la nature humaine telle qu'elle était ...? (102). The theater, which cultivates illusion in order to express ideas about truth, furnished artists and philosophers with a rich solution to this dilemma. Although it was to prove intolerable to the mind of the late Enlightenment,[2] the rococo found in a decorative ideal a sophisticated way to speak of the real (Levey 52). Because the theater manifests this decorative ideal most completely, it informed the rococo movement with regard both to *forme* and to *fond*. An analysis of narrative structures in Riccoboni's rococo text reveals its hidden theatrical architecture.

If letters gave writers and readers a sense of the real, theatricality embellished epistolary writing with a "decorative ideal" (Levey 52). The letters in *Juliette Catesby* unfold like an epistolary comedy or letter-play. The text begins *in medias res* with a first-person account of a flight from London to the English countryside:

LETTRE PREMIÈRE

Mardi, de Summerhill

C'est au grand trot de six forts chevaux, avec des relais bien disposés, l'air de l'empressement, que je vais très vite, accompagnée de gens dont je me soucie peu, chez d'autres dont je ne me soucie point du tout. J'abandonne mes amis les plus chers; je vous quitte, vous que j'aime si tendrement! Eh pourquoi ce départ,

---

[2] Michael Fried explains that "the reaction against the Rococo ... began [around] 1747 ... its basic features are well known: a turning away from the exquisite, sensuous, intimately decorative painting that had held the field for roughly thirty years; and an insistence on the need to return to what were perceived as the high seriousness, elevated morality, and timeless esthetic principles of the great art of the past, by which was meant the sculpture of the ancients and the paintings of certain canonical sixteenth- and seventeenth-century masters" (35). Nicolas Poussin was lauded and emulated as such a master. Michael Levey adds that the anti-rococo movement was based on accusations of a "lack of truthfulness [and a] disregard of the classical canons ... [i]t remained very much a Southern European world [and perhaps for this reason] required a suspension of disbelief [that] was hardest to achieve in France; before such critical audiences the spell seldom worked" (51-52).

> cette hâte? Pourquoi me presser d'arriver où je ne désire point d'être? Pour m'éloigner ... de qui? de Milord d'Ossery.... (7)

The description of rapid physical movement in this opening letter reinforces the energetic psychological process here at work. From the start, the reader learns that Juliette is torn from her amical and amorous attachments; the ensuing correspondence strives above all to *close up*, with each successive letter, this physical and psychological *éloignement*. In addition, the opening letter carries within it the *arrival point* of the entire correspondence: speaking of d'Ossery, Juliette exclaims "[q]ue sa femme a dû regretter la vie!" (8). Now the reader cannot grasp this reference until the very end of the text, at which point s/he learns (by reading the embedded "Histoire de Milord d'Ossery") that the death of Jenny Montfort allows d'Ossery to quit his *devoir* in the name of *amour*. By the end of the correspondence, the reader may well have forgotten the *clue* given in the first letter. No matter, for the spiral rococo structure allows for apprehension at multiple points: what is missed will always return.

After the abrupt start in Letter 1, which signals a broken equilibrium according to the dramatic tradition, additional introductory letters serve as a *scène d'exposition*. Each of Letters 2-7 reveals further movement in space and time: "Mercredi, de chez Sir John Warthy," "Jeudi, de chez Milord d'Erby," "Vendredi, de chez votre très humble adorateur, Sir Georges Howard," "Samedi, du Château d'Hastings," "Dimanche, à Winchester." Letter 7 corresponds to the seventh day of the week and it is at Winchester that the heroine will rest and write: until the final letter announcing her marriage to d'Ossery, each letter will bear the heading "A Winchester." Rococo movement therefore characterizes this theatrical exposition, entirely subverting the Classical unities of time and place.

Once settled in her gracious surroundings, Juliette provides her friend (and the reader) with a description of her entourage; her report prolongs the exposition:

> Vous me demandez ce que je fais, avec qui je suis, quels sont ceux qui me plaisent davantage ... [n]ous sommes ici quinze ou seize habitants de Londres, sans compter la Noblesse des environs qui abonde au Château. Ce grand cercle m'étourdit plus qu'il ne m'amuse. (Letter 8, 24)

What follows in this passage is a series of verbal portraits representing *points* in this "grand cercle": there is Milord Winchester, "[qui] dessine correctement, peint de petits écrans qui ne sont ni laids ni jolis et fait avec facilité des vers détestables"; Milady Winchester, "aimable ... belle et bien faite"; the Countess of Bristol, "[b]elle en tout point, belle depuis le matin jusqu'au soir"; and Sir Manley, "... simple, uni; un véritable Anglais" (pp. 24-27). Together, these characters form the community within which Juliette will *play out* her conflict between personal honor and desire by writing to the absent Henriette. Moreover, the community will both help and hinder her in her search to reconcile the conflict: while her servant Abraham helps by delivering her letters and bringing her mail, the clumsy suitors Sir Henry and Sir James often interrupt her thought process and intercept her as she strolls along the grounds:

> Mais on entre ... qui est-ce? ... Eh qui pourrait-ce être que Sir Henry? ... Pourquoi faut-il que je le reçoive? Quel droit a-t-il de m'ennuyer? (Letter 8, 25)

> Heureusement débarrassée de Sir Henry ... j'ai voulu profiter du plaisir de me promener seule. Au détour d'une allée ... j'ai trouvé Sir James. Il m'avait suivie sans se laisser apercevoir; sa rencontre m'a extrêmement déplu ...Sir James s'est enfoncé dans le bois et votre folle amie a coupé par une petite allée pour n'être point vue; elle se hâte de vous écrire.... (Letter 26, 81-82)

The detours and garden hedges through which Juliette zigzags reflect a mode of writing that *hedges* univocal meaning and refuses categorization. This form of writing represents a literary rococo to the extent that it presents a profusion of generic codes: in blending theatrical conceits with novelistic purpose, Riccoboni magnifies the poetic potential of each. As Carol Sherman points out, the attempt to speak of a literary rococo is legitimized by the fact that "[l]e rococo lui-même entretient l'idée du transfert d'un genre ou d'un domaine à l'autre" ("Diderot" 253).

The role of Henriette within the narrative further demonstrates how dramatic traditions (both French and Italian) inform *Juliette Catesby*. Henriette's role is that of confidante and she fulfills it with great finesse, since she performs the one action required of her–she stays away. Unlike the scenic confidante who stays close by the protagonist's side, the epistolary confidante must remain at a distance in order to ensure that the protagonist writes. Emotional intimacy is predicated upon separation in space and time–this is perhaps the greatest paradox of epistolary writing and reflects the Enlightenment taste for complexity. In *Epistolarity*, Janet Altman has provided a lengthy analysis of the ways in which "the letter novel appropriated [the confidante] from classical theater" and I shall not restate the obvious here (46). What I would like to add is the special mirroring that Riccoboni sets up between the heroine and her *aimable amie*, for it again illustrates rococo purpose. This mirroring operates with regard to proper names and becomes evident in the title of the text:

LETTRES
DE
MILADY JULIETTE CATESBY
A
MILADY HENRIETTE CAMPLEY,
SON AMIE

Within the very title of the text one may appreciate the extent to which Riccoboni's art reflects the rococo esthetic. The principle at work here is what Carol Sherman has called *atectonicité* and may be defined as near-symmetry, a feeling of being "balanced without being equilibrated" ("Space and Time" 230). Near-symmetry is apparent in the fact that protagonist and confidant have almost the same name: if I strip away those letters that do *not* mirror each other exactly, I am still left with "Milady ***ette Ca****y." Linguistic near-symmetry finds its echo in the semantic prepositional connectors "de" and "à": the letters are *from/by* Juliette and *for/to* Henriette. In this way the affective connection between the two women is semantically inscribed.

TOUT EST PARDONNÉ: THE LETTER AS *DEUS EX MACHINA*

Through her faithful correspondence addressed to Henriette, Juliette slowly writes her way out of the dilemma imposed by d'Ossery's infidelity and subsequent demand for forgiveness. Henriette's letters (of which the reader remains deprived) become a kind of protean mirror for Juliette, reflecting images of herself that are at times flattering, at times disconcerting for her. Henriette enjoys the privilege of total information: she reads not only those letters addressed to her but also all those that Juliette writes and receives. In her elect position within the correspondence Henriette seemingly anticipates Laclos's Mme de Merteuil–nearly every epistle passes through her hands. However, while Merteuil seeks to destroy affective ties, Henriette strives to mend those already broken: their motivations are as different as their functions are similar.

Despite Henriette's loyal advice and confidence, Juliette remains perplexed and cannot reconcile honor and desire: she states her conflict in very succinct terms approximately mid-way through the correspondence (page 85 of the 175-page Desjonquères edition): "était-ce pour être suivie que je fuyais? aurais-eu je la bassesse de désirer?" Here is the *noeud* of this letter-play that Riccoboni appropriately places at the center of the text. What follows this psychological knot is a slow, epistolary *dénouement*: d'Ossery tries first to see Juliette and then to write to her in an attempt to justify his behavior. Juliette refuses his presence and resists his words; all the while, she sends Henriette transcribed copies of letters written and sent. It is evident that Henriette has a hand in bringing about the lovers' reconciliation, as Juliette's responses make clear:

> La lettre de Milord d'Ossery vous a touchée; ma réponse vous paraît très *haute*; vous n'approuvez point cet excès de sévérité. Allons, poursuivez, ma chère Henriette, chagrinez- moi aussi. (Letter 26,109)

Although Juliette claims to resist d'Ossery's efforts as well as Henriette's approval of them, she soon admits–as always, in a letter to Henriette–that her resistance masks a desire to succumb: "un reproche est le préliminaire d'un traité de paix" (Letter 33, 134). Masking, as I have suggested, leads the couple to the truth: d'Ossery has always loved the young widow and married Jenny Montfort only out of duty. This masking manifests itself in a literal sense (d'Ossery shows up in disguise at the *bal masqué*) and in an abstract one (Letter 35 serves as a mask made of words).

Letter 35 constitutes Juliette's letter to Henriette, in which she has folded the *cahier* written to her by d'Ossery. This cahier in turn contains the *histoire intercalée* entitled "Histoire de Milord d'Ossery," in which is embedded a brief note from Jenny Montfort to Milord. The rococo structure of this Letter merits further consideration and I shall return to it shortly. It functions thematically as a *deus ex machina*: it explains everything, and after it is read (by both Juliette and Henriette) Juliette forgives. In response to his long-winded plea she writes a brief *billet* in which she says "[s]i vous voulez vous rendre à Erford, j'y reverrai le Comte d'Ossery avec ce plaisir vif qu'on sent en retrouvant un ami que l'on croyait perdu pour jamais" (Letter 37, 171). The dénouement is complete and ends on the soft rhetorical note of the *litote*. In addition, the closing letters of the text echo the comic tradition, as Janet Altman explains:

> At the end of [the text] ... new voices (other than Juliette's) are heard. Letters from Mylord d'Ossery, Mylady d'Ossery (Juliette), and Mylady d'Ormond [Juliette's cousin] follow each other in rapid succession, each inviting Henriette to join them for the wedding festivities. This sudden proliferation of letter writers resembles the final scene in classical comedy, where all the characters are brought together on stage to celebrate the lovers' marriage. An actress herself, Mme Riccoboni simply translated the conventional theatrical denouement into epistolary form to create the same sense of closure. (150)

While it is true that Riccoboni closes her text with a flurry of letters recapitulating the Classical *rassemblement final*, the final scene of writing is not in my view a simple transposition from stage to page. Rather this transcodification (from the dramatic code to the novelistic code) entails a complex gesture of generic blending that exemplifies Enlightenment ambiguity and, in so doing, anticipates the romantic notion of the *mélange des genres*.

The closing letter (Letter 37) cultivates the *idea(l)* of presence even as it insists upon absence; if we look carefully at the joyous ensemble we realize that someone has been left out–Henriette. Her absence may be explained in terms of epistolary technique: in order for the letters describing the marriage to be written it is necessary that she not attend. However, what I observe in the final utterances is a play on joy and sorrow, presence and absence, that goes beyond technique. Behind the *appearance* of a joyous marriage Riccoboni insists upon the theme of incommunicability that she has cultivated throughout the text. Typical of the Enlightenment, transparency is an ideal that may be *performed*–on the Island of Cythera, in the English countryside, at Clarens–but never truly maintained. Riccoboni hints at the cloudy transparency of Juliette's union to d'Ossery by showing how differently they describe their wedding day: d'Ossery calls it "le jour à jamais fortuné" while the young bride relates to Henriette that "on m'a mariée si vite, si vite, que je crois de bonne foi que le mariage ne vaut rien" (173-174). Juliette's use of the impersonal phrase "on m'a mariée"–in which she is the object–suggests that she is an object of exchange within an economy of desire. Indeed, her cousin Milady d'Ormond confirms the terms of the exchange in the subsequent note: "[o]ui, je l'ai mariée au Seigneur d'Angleterre le plus aimable; le mariage est bon, je vous assure, et aucune des parties contractantes n'a envie de le rompre" (174).

In this final epistolary scene Riccoboni speaks of transparency as an ideal form of communication that may be performed but not experienced. The performance brings joy but that joy is short-lived, as the final letter authored by Juliette makes clear:

Milady d'Ossery

On vous attend avec impatience ici: point de fêtes, de bals sans ma chère Henriette; je dirais point de plaisirs si la personne qui suit ma plume des yeux n'était pas un peu jalouse de ma tendre amitié. (175)

Here jealousy overshadows the joyous nuptial event and threatens the friendship of Juliette and Henriette. In an effort to ignore this *ombre*, Juliette calls for more parties and balls, seeking in theatrical diversion a way to conquer her aversion for "[ceux qui] étaient tous unis contre [elle]" (173). The shadows that Riccoboni throws on the final scene of this epistolary comedy destabilize the sense of closure, rendering it equivocal. The allusions to Juliette's lack of agency, Henriette's persistent absence, and d'Ossery's jealousy subvert the happy ending and suggest that this nuptial union is more like an unhappy beginning.

Rather than effect a simple translation from the dramatic code to the epistolary code, Riccoboni stages in letters a sophisticated exploration into the kinds of relationships–marriage, friendship–that define communities. Because Juliette's conflict remains unresolved (she says in Letter 37 that she was led to marriage as to a trap) and because the appearance of resolution gives rise to a new conflict (the threat to female intimacy), the text closes on an ambivalent note. The community has evolved yet tensions remain; future losses are foreshadowed even as present gain is celebrated.

I have suggested that a concern with community is a defining feature of the rococo in both painting and literature and that it may stem from the etymology of the term. In the decorative arts, the rococo employs a profusion of figures and creates false supplements to visual abundance through *trompe l'oeil* techniques. In painting (I am again thinking of Watteau) the theme of *communitas* predominates: assemblies of figures both human and divine recall the decorative patterns of leaves and shells. In *Lettres de Juliette Catesby* the "quinze ou seize habitants de Londres" (the inexact number is true to another rococo quality–asymmetry) *arrange* themselves by playing certain parts including those of friend, lover, wife, and mother.[3] These roles allow the community to believe in itself as a whole–they serve as a kind of *trompe-le-coeur*. Nevertheless, if rococo plenitude is suggestive of the idea of society, it must be said to be a society in the making, a community *à devenir* that defines itself through tension and change. Like the epistolary novel–itself a literary genre in the *act* of becoming–the rococo reflects a society deeply engaged in stating new truths from behind a mask and in re-shaping itself through *serious play*.

THE SERPENTINE LINE

In my analysis of *Lettres de Juliette Catesby* I have demonstrated how theatricality informs the diegesis and structures epistolary

---

[3] In his "Histoire" (Letter 35) d'Ossery reveals that Jenny Montfort gave birth to a baby girl:

> Milady d'Ossery donna le jour à une fille: sa vue passa dans mon coeur le seul mouvement de joie que j'aie senti loin de vous. Aimable petite innocente! combien de fois l'ai-je baignée de mes larmes, en m'applaudissant pourtant d'avoir rempli mes devoirs à son égard! Ah, que de tendresse elle devrait à son père, si elle savait jamais à quel prix il lui donna son nom! (156-157)

As part of his exhortation to Juliette he pleads with her to accept his daughter along with him: "Aimez ma fille, aimez-la...." (162). It is to be assumed that in marrying d'Ossery Juliette will adopt this little girl as her own. Her reconfiguration within this society therefore involves her transition from the "unnatural" position of widow to the "natural" roles of wife and mother.

form. Because it bears the imprint of theatrical structures, this epistolary work reflects a generic hybridization that is characteristic of the rococo generally (Sherman "Diderot" 253). To conclude, I would like to explore the overriding structure of the text in order to demonstrate its rococo architecture. This architecture will reveal itself to be in accordance with the predominant visual ideal of the pictorial rococo–the serpentine line. This curvilinear ideal was theorized by William Hogarth in his 1753 treatise entitled *The Analysis of Beauty* and I shall consider his contribution here.

Many art historians and literary scholars have considered the notion of the serpentine line in order to speak of the rococo in visual art and in literature. I first came across the term in Jean Rousset's well-known chapter on epistolary form in *Forme et signification*: speaking of Laclos's *Les Liaisons dangereuses*, he writes that with this form "[o]n évoque la ligne serpentine, la seule ligne de beauté selon Hogarth" (87). Considering the esthetic affinity between Marivaux and Watteau, Robert Tomlinson has written convincingly of the rapport between the serpentine line in Watteau's paintings and the verbal arabesque in the plays of Marivaux: this rapport is based on a contingency between "le rythme d'une phrase et la courbe d'une arabesque" (139).[4] Lastly, art historians stress the importance of this shape in contemplating the meaning of the rococo.

Although Hogarth was not the first artist to theorize the serpentine line,[5] Jack Lindsay explains that "he applied the idea of the ser-

---

[4] Tomlinson specifies that "l'arabesque peut constituer un point de coïncidence entre la structure du tableau [de Watteau] et celle de la pièce [de Marivaux], à condition de reconnaître que les mouvements de l'arabesque plastique et de l'arabesque verbale doivent s'élaborer selons leurs propres lois formelles" (139). Tomlinson does not clarify what these "formal laws" might be; however, Carol Sherman's article on the rhetoric of rococo sheds light on the question. She explains that this "formal law" dividing the plastic and verbal arts goes back to an eighteenth-century view that "la littérature se développe dans le temps, les arts plastiques dans l'espace." She goes on to free up this division by asking "les arts plastiques, à y regarder de plus près, ne peuvent-ils pas en effet comporter une vitalité qui les range dans la temporalité?" (252). Certainly the answer is yes, and given the emergence in poetry of the *calligramme* (which dates *not* to Apollinaire but rather to the eighteenth-century poet François-Charles Panard) it may be said that the verbal arts deploy their signs spatially as well as temporally. Mallarmé's *Un coup de dés*, like the *calligramme*, illustrates the poet's fascination with a *mise en espace* of verbal signs; it may be read as a pictorial exploration of the sign's dissolution.

[5] Jack Lindsay points out that Hogarth was ignorant of certain artists who had theorized the arabesque line before him:

pentine line in a new way, with a fullness and subtlety of range" (171). The *Analysis of Beauty* brought him fame and carried his name abroad; Peter Quennell confirms that the esthetic treatise was translated into German and French and that it was "both attacked and plagiarized by Diderot" (235). Although Riccoboni was fluent in English and was an anglophile, there can be no assurance as to whether she read the essay: I am making my argument for Hogarth's influence on the age generally–an age that is known for its internationalism (Levey 55). I am, furthermore, conceptualizing his Line of Beauty in view of his own conception: "he knew that the line was an abstraction" (Lindsay 181).

Hogarth's innovation was his empiricism; he was able to associate his abstractions with familiar objects in the real world. Although his Line of Beauty was an *ideal* it could be glimpsed in natural and human forms (Quennell 224). Chapter Nine of the *Analysis* presents its form: it is a waving serpentine line whose proportions are perfect. The object chosen by Hogarth to illustrate this ideal line is the unassuming whale-bone corset or "stay":

> A still more perfect idea of the effects of the precise waving-line, and of those lines that deviate from it, may be conceived by the row of stays [depicted in his Figure 53] ... [e]very whale-bone of a good stay must be made to bend in this manner: for the whole stay, when put close together behind, is truly a shell of well-varied contents, and its surface of course a fine form; so that if a line, or the lace were to be drawn or brought from the top of the lacing of the stay behind, round the body, and down to the bottom peak of the stomacher; it would form such a perfect, precise serpentine-line, as it has been shown, round the cone, figure 26 in plate 1. (49)

In this passage we may see the predominant features of Hogarth's conception of beauty: beauty is above all an expression of move-

---

If he had read John Elsum's *The Art of Painting after the Italian Manner* of 1703, he would have found the serpentine line there. He could further have cited Testelin, Dupuy de Grez, De Lairesse, and Jonathan Richardson ... However, Hogarth had in effect covered himself [since he mentions Lomazzo's treatment of the serpentine line]. (171)

Lindsay makes it clear that although artists before Hogarth had spoken of the undulating line, Hogarth surpassed his predecessors through his empirical observations.

ment (the waving line) and variety (the corset is a visual expression of composed variety). Jack Lindsay further observes that for Hogarth, "[v]ariety is the result of a fusion of intricacy and simplification, and is an active principle, compared to a kind of chase or pursuit in which the artist is himself involved. Form is thus inseparable from movement" (167). It is relevant to my thesis that Hogarth dwells upon the characters of the *commedia dell'arte* in his essay in order to relate human movement to the serpentine line. He expresses childlike admiration for the Italian theater, which he calls "the genius of that nation," and lauds the character of Harlequin (among others) for his "little, quick movements of the head, hands, and feet, some of which shoot out as it were from the body in straight lines, or are twirled about in little circles" (148-149).

Hogarth distinguishes between what he calls the Line of Beauty and the Line of Grace. Whereas the former is a line that waves in two dimensions, the latter is a three-dimensional waving line that twists. Once again, the illustration of such an elevated esthetic is to be found in common objects: a ribbon winding around a stick,[6] a seashell, a kitchen spool:

---

[6] Hogarth's stick-and-ribbon ornament, which illustrates his Line of Grace, is an object that fascinated Charles Baudelaire—the thyrsus. Webster defines the thyrsus as "a staff tipped with a pine cone and sometimes entwined with ivy or vine leaves, which Dionysus, the satyrs, etc. were represented as carrying." It is not hard to see in this object the union of masculine and feminine imagery. In his prose poem entitled "Le Thyrse," Baudelaire defines the object poetically and makes of it an emblem of his theory of *correspondances*:

> Qu'est-ce qu'un thyrse? Selon le sens moral et poétique, c'est un emblème sacerdotal dans la main des prêtres et des prêtresses célébrant la divinité dont ils sont les interprètes et les serviteurs. Mais physiquement ce n'est qu'un bâton, un pur bâton, perche à houblon, tuteur de vigne, sec, dur et droit. Autour de ce bâton, dans des méandres capricieux, se jouent et folâtrent des tiges et des fleurs, celles-si sinueuses et fuyardes, celles-là perchées comme des cloches ou des coupes renversées. Et une gloire étonnante jaillit de cette complexité de lignes et de couleurs, tendres ou éclatantes. Ne dirait-on que la ligne courbe et spirale font leur cour à la ligne droite et dansent autour dans une muette adoration? ... Ligne droite et ligne arabesque, intention et expression, roideur de la volonté, sinuosité du verbe, unité du but, variété des moyens, amalgame tout-puissant et indivisible du génie, quel analyste aura le détestable courage de vous diviser et de vous séparer? (172-73)

Here this object expresses the ideal of difference effaced since the straight line communes with the arabesque. Baudelaire's prose poem re-states in Symbolist terms the fusion of opposites that Hogarth had incorporated in his conception of beauty.

> As a child [Hogarth had] discovered the mystery of form movement through the vanishing spiral of the turning kitchen-jack. The line twists and curves away in order to be reborn at the point where it began; and because the line is spiral it involves bulk, volume, spatial depth. (Lindsay 168)

The Line of Grace is therefore an "uninterrupted flowing twist" (60) or a "continued waving flow" (64). This form of beauty is to be found, the artist explains, in such unassuming objects as the horn of plenty (or cornucopia) or human bones.

It pleases the human eye and mind, he writes, because it "gives play to the imagination" (52). Here the affinity between epistolary form and his theory begins to emerge. As I have earlier discussed, epistolary writing requires that the reader fill in the blanks and imagine what is evoked but not explicitly stated. Like a rococo seashell whose contours suggest that there is more than meets the eye, letter-texts present *contours of meaning* and invite the reader to fill those contours by imagining events unseen and letters unwritten. Like the Lines, epistolary writing lays bare the structure of its composition and, in so doing, incites the reader to enter into the apprehension of pure form.

Serpentine Composition in *Lettres de Juliette Catesby*

The architecture of *Juliette Catesby* may be said to illustrate the Line of Grace in that it exhibits serpentine structures. The idea of *interrelated movement* is what leads me to speak of spiraling in these two letters: in the narrative, each turn is contingent upon the last. The reading-process itself also contributes to the notion of spiraling; as the pages turn, the reader turns back in time and then doubles back to the present moment of interpretation, moving with the protagonist in a non-linear narrative of events. The most subtle operation of the spiral in this text occurs in Letter 1: writing to Henriette of her flight from London, Juliette alludes to the deceased wife of d'Ossery—"[q]ue sa femme a dû regretter la vie!" (8). Here, as I have previously mentioned, the entire correspondence wraps around from end to beginning: in this initial letter lies the seed of resolution that will not be sown until d'Ossery's lengthy explanation in Letter 35. Between Letter 1 and the final Letter (37), spiral structure continues to inform the work and reflects the heroine's *état d'étourdissement*.

In addition to Letter 1, there are two other significant instances of spiraling in the text: Letter 14 and Letter 35. The process of reading these two letters resembles that of taking apart a set of Chinese boxes: inside each letter lies another. In addition, both letters provide significant and new information that alters the way in which the conflict and resolution unfold. Letter 14 begins on page forty-three of the Desjonquères edition and ends on page seventy-six. It begins as a letter from Juliette to Henriette in which she encloses–for Henriette's perusal–a letter that she has written to Milord Carlile in response to his request that Juliette pardon d'Ossery and accept d'Ossery's friendship. Juliette passes on this letter secretively, writing to Henriette "je ne voudrais pas qu'une autre vît cette Histoire ... [j]'ai passé une partie de la nuit à l'écrire" (43). Upon reading the enclosed letter, the reader–both intradiegetic and extradiegetic–discovers within it the *histoire intercalée* entitled "Histoire de Milady Juliette Catesby et de Milord d'Ossery." This embedded story tells a tale of desire from Juliette's point of view and is redolent of *La Princesse de Clèves*.[7] True to rococo taste, this embedded tale itself embeds a short note; deep within its structure lies a transcription of a note written by Milord d'Ossery to Juliette in which d'Ossery announces but does not explain his abrupt departure.

The structure of Letter 14 may be set forth visually in the following way:

---

[7] Juliette's story resembles that of *La Princesse de Clèves*. Like Lafayette, Riccoboni emphasizes the role of the gaze within a community in which women are displayed like so many theatrical objects. Within this theater of desire, the female subject who wishes for *agency* finds herself open to shame; dissimulation therefore emerges as a strategy allowing the female subject to express desire while protecting her name. Juliette writes, for instance, that in the early stages of her relationship with d'Ossery "je veillais sans cesse sur moi-même pour cacher ... mon trouble" (52). As it is the case in Lafayette's text, the gaze betrays unwanted or forbidden desire: "je ne pus me défendre, en regardant le Comte [d'Ossery], de ce trouble, de cet embarras qui dit si bien ce qu'on s'efforce de taire" (54).

Serpentine Structure of Letter 14

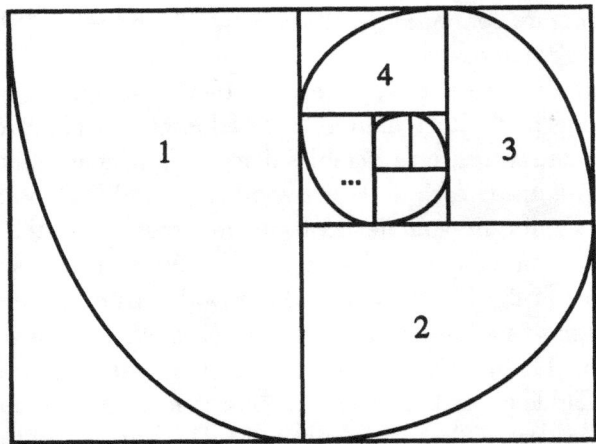

1) Letter from Juliette to Henriette (pages 43-44)
2) Letter from Juliette to Milord Carlile (pages 44-46 and 76)
3) Histoire de Milady Juliette Catesby et de Milord d'Ossery (pages 46-65 and 66-76)
4) Note from Milord d'Ossery to Juliette (pages 65-66)

    It is noteworthy that in Letter 14 information becomes more dense as the structure of the letter becomes more serpentine. By the time the reader has read through the embedded story with its interpolated note, s/he has learned that Juliette truly desired d'Ossery, that after his departure her brother died, and that she used mourning as a mask to hide the deeper grief caused by her lover's betrayal. Such a density of expression is absent in the rest of the correspondence; in the straightforward letters Juliette's confidential reflections are balanced by accounts of minor events and conversations.

    The second spiral structure occurs in Letter 35 near the end of the text and reveals a structure similar to that of Letter 14: it begins on page 137 and then unfolds its four-tiered nested design for thirty pages. Juliette writes of her longing for d'Ossery when her servant Abraham enters her quarters carrying "tout un cahier écrit de la main de Milord" (138). Saying that she is "burning to read," Juliette closes her note by asking "qu'est-ce donc qu'il me dit? Vous le saurez dès que j'aurai parcouru ce cahier" (138). Just below those words Riccoboni presents the reader(s) with the contents of the cahier. First there is a letter from d'Ossery to Juliette in which he justifies the act of writing; following that brief explanation there is the lengthy "Histoire de Milord d'Ossery." Here we have the complement to Juliette's tale as told in Letter 14: this second *histoire intercalée* tells the story of their relationship from his point of view and goes on to describe the "fatal adventure" that followed his self-imposed exile from Juliette, whom he calls the "ornament of the female sex" (143, 141). This story, as I have already suggested, serves as an epistolary *deus ex machina*; after it is received and read, Juliette forgives and the two are wed.

Structurally, Letter 35 emerges as a kind of mirror image of Letter 14: where Letter 14 tells Juliette's story, it tells the same story from the male point of view. Embedded in d'Ossery's "Histoire" is a transcription of the note Jenny Montfort wrote to him; it serves as a kind of epistolary *proof* that d'Ossery was bound to Jenny out of duty.

The spiral of Letter 35 may also be set forth visually:

Serpentine Structure of Letter 35

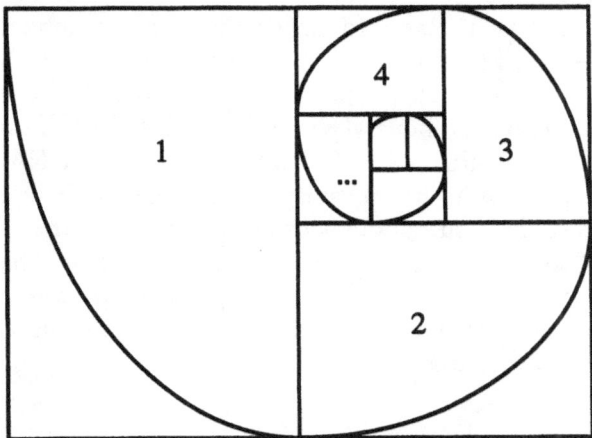

1) Letter from Juliette to Henriette (pages 137-38 and 167)
2) Letter from Milord d'Ossery to Milady Catesby (pages 138-139)
3) Histoire de Milord d'Ossery (pages 139-51 and 152-66)
4) Letter from Jenny Montfort to Milord, Compte d'Ossery (pages 151-52)

In this text, reason is the vanishing point within the spiral of desire. The center of the spiral in Letter 14 (the note from d'Ossery to Juliette) effected a perplexing rupture between the couple while the center of the spiral in Letter 35 (the note from Jenny to d'Ossery) *justifies* that rupture and therefore brings it to an end. By constructing such elaborate patterns and arranging their disposition symmetrically within the diegesis, Riccoboni amplifies the central conflict of the text: incommunicability caused by infidelity.

In the architecture of this text I observe something of Hogarth's Line of Grace. My observation is based on the spatial movement that the reading process suggests: Letters 14 and 35 cause the reader to *turn* deeper and deeper *with* the protagonist and toward a revelation that is almost lost within the maze of psychological twists and turns. Within this maze (depicted literally in the garden scene in Letter 26) heroine and hero express themselves in *eddies* of feeling, whirls of thought: Juliette speaks of her wish to "[s]'abîmer dans [s]a douleur" (68) and d'Ossery relates how "[u]ne espèce de frénésie [lui] ôta l'usage de [s]es sens" (155). By requiring the extradiegetic reader to navigate a signifying system characterized by coherent disorder, Riccoboni invites him or her to participate in the creative process. The need for imaginative participation on the part of the reader is loyal to Hogarth's esthetic: beauty is to be apprehended through an active reflection of pure form. Active reflection, furthermore, comes about when the reader/beholder *fills in* the object of contemplation–a sea-shell, a text, a model of DNA–through the exercise of his or her imagination. The Line of Grace expresses the spirit of the rococo; both animate Riccoboni's *Lettres de Milady Juliette Catesby à Milady Henriette Campley, son amie*. This spirit is spiritedness itself, expressed in the serpentine line that symbolizes "the resolution of entangled tensions, pulls, conflicting and interacting forms" (Lindsay 173).

VI

MEDIATING DESIRE: THE VEIL IN *LA NOUVELLE HÉLOÏSE* AND IN *LETTRES DE MISTRESS FANNI BUTLERD*

Epistolary writing combines narrative, dramatic, and poetic codes in such a way that it incorporates all genres while privileging none. The semiotic *sum* of these codes is greater than its parts; the letter is at once prose poem, miniature narrative, and theatrical tableau. In the monophonic register, blank space, brevity, and the lack of omniscient narration foster a kind of generic (con)fusion. The nature of Lyric in the literature of the Enlightenment has everything to do with this mixing of form; in this sense, it anticipates the principle of *le mélange des genres* theorized by Madame de Staël and put into practice by writers like Hugo (*Hernani*) and Nerval (*Les Filles du feu*). Epistolary writing evolved in part as a response to the socio-political conditions under which the eighteenth-century writer toiled, as Georges May has shown, and may therefore be identified as an esthetic strategy. Little by little, however, the very obstacles that gave rise to the epistolary vogue—censorship, denigration of lyric verse, the dilemma of *réalisme/moralisme*—were turned to artistic advantage. The dilemma, in other words, inspired the writer even as it restricted him or her and questions of *forme* gradually meshed with those of *fond*.

As the eighteenth century progressed, literature began to reflect the changing reality of an early modern society. Instead of dictating to the reader/spectator, the writer was (somewhat) free to depict individual experience and to comment on society. Montesquieu's *Lettres persanes* (1721) and Graffigny's *Lettres d'une Péruvienne* (1747) exemplify the *liberté masquée* made possible by a new conception of literature as an instrument of symbolic *mediation* between the artist-philosopher and the people. Rather than drawing a boundary between the King and his subjects, literature and visual art mediated *between* self and society.

The concept of mediation lends itself well to a discussion of post-classical representation; in this chapter I shall explore this concept primarily in an esthetic sense but also (and first) in a historical one. The etymological (r)evolution of the verb *to mediate* holds interesting ramifications for the study of epistolary writing and I shall discuss it shortly. In a historical sense, I am using the term to describe how art in the Enlightenment became the medium for social, political, and esthetic change rather than a script ensuring the status quo. Because written and visual texts served to *narrate change*,[1] they mediated between the old (Louis XIV's reign) and the new (*La Régence*). Now to suggest that the artist strove to articulate such a transition is not to ignore the difficulty or complexity of the effort. As May has shown, the attempt to mediate between old and new, the real and the ideal, was fraught with tension and uncertainty. Indeed, one of the paradoxes of post-classical representation is that it seems to have derived life from the very forces that threatened its survival.

It is paradoxical that Enlightenment writers upheld rational discourses and at the same time invented a new cult of feeling called *sensibilité*. Indeed, the works of Rousseau and Diderot fluctuate between reasoned or logical argumentation and sentimental fiction. Throughout the century, the written word ceaselessly mediated the laborious transition from past to present. Often, a plea for change was incorporated within the story itself; Diderot's *La Religieuse*, Graffigny's *Lettres d'une Péruvienne*, and Riccoboni's *Lettres de Mistress Fanni Butlerd*, for example, all criticize the socio-political conditions under which eighteenth-century women lived and propose an enlightened reevaluation of them. Rousseau's preface to *La Nouvelle Héloïse* illustrates the way in which philosophical questions play themselves out in the medium of fiction:

> Il faut des spectacles dans les grandes villes, et des romans aux peuples corrompus. J'ai vu les moeurs de mon temps, et j'ai publié ces lettres ... la correspondance entière est-elle une fiction?

---

[1] See Ronald Rosbottom's article "Narrating the Regency" for an insightful discussion of the ways in which Marivaux's written texts and Watteau's visual texts speak of "the need for a new order of signs and tropes to represent [the] still inchoate values ... of the early Enlightenment" (343).

> Gens du monde, que vous importe? C'est sûrement une fiction pour vous ... [q]uiconque veut se résoudre à lire ces lettres doit s'armer de patience ... ceux qui les écrivent ne sont pas des beaux-esprits, des académiciens, des philosophes, mais des provinciaux, des étrangers, des solitaires, de jeunes gens, presque des enfants, qui, dans leurs imaginations romanesques, prennent pour de la philosophie les honnêtes délires de leur cerveau. (3)

In his preface Rousseau introduces the impossible rapport between the real and the ideal that will inform the entire work. He contrasts his real audience—*les gens du monde*—with his ideal reader, whom he envisions would be "armed with patience" and appreciative of the childlike qualities of his *solitaires*. Rousseau is therefore forging a rapport between the creator (self) and consumer (Other) of his book: "Ce livre ... convient à très peu de lecteurs ... à qui plaira-t-il donc? Peut-être à moi seul" (3). The book mediates between artist and society just as its fictive letters *depict* an ideal—and thus impossible—mediation between "deux amants, habitants d'une petite ville au pied des Alpes" (5).

During the Enlightenment, the historical relation between individual and society was regulated in large part by the widespread diffusion of printed matter; in epistolary texts, subject-object relations are similarly mediated by the written word. Elizabeth Cook confirms that epistolary writing "took shape in the early eighteenth century along with the forms and institutions of a developing print culture.... the letter-narrative figures this historical moment between manuscript and print, private correspondence and published text" (2). The operation by which this transition *figured* itself, I add, is that of mediation—a constant if not always organized *zig-zag* between experience and representation, between real and ideal. The *mediating* word, epitomized by the letter that literally traces a path between self and other, appears to have moved French society into the modern age.

The Veil

The veil figures prominently in many epistolary narratives of the Enlightenment; in a general sense I read it as a visual sign designating the female body as the uncanny site of alterity. Unlike the linguistic sign that stands in for an absent referent, the veil conceals a referent–the female body–that is somehow *too present* while at the same time revealing that body's so-called lack. The veil simultaneously reveals and conceals a kind of *presence of lack* that is eminently feminine.

As an emblem for what is *not there*, the veil suggests not only sexual difference but also, in the eyes of the more sympathetic *philosophes*, the *equality* that women lack. In *La Religieuse*, for example, Diderot evokes the religious veil to decry women's lack of agency in society. As a symbolic illustration of his conviction that "on est esclave dans le cloître," Diderot has his protagonist emerge from behind her veil and take a free, if humble, role in society (54). And in *Lettres persanes*, Roxane's suicide may be read as a declaration of freedom from the cloak of servitude imposed upon her by Usbek: "Oui, je t'ai trompé ... [c]omment as-tu pensé que je fusse assez crédule pour m'imaginer que je ne fusse dans le Monde que pour adorer tes caprices? ... [c]e langage, sans doute, te paraît nouveau" (252-53). Her language of protest certainly appears new when compared to that of her literary ancestors like the Portugese nun and the Princess of Clèves. Nevertheless, while Montesquieu would seem to make a claim for woman's liberty, the reader infers that the price of liberty is death.

Although Diderot and Montesquieu critique woman's status as Other within the socio-political system that they observed, they persist in veiling woman's sexuality. In their novels, both philosophers relegate feminine sexuality to the obscure spaces of the convent and the seraglio. Diderot codes feminine sexuality as something marginal and unknowable through his allusive depiction of homosexual relations. Moreover, Suzanne's entire narrative represents a lengthy epistle addressed to M. le marquis de Croismare, the aim of which is to reinstate the young woman within a heterosexual and paternalistic matrix: "Monsieur, hâtez-vous de me secourir" (206). In a somewhat different scenario, Montesquieu marginalizes the desiring female subject by placing her beyond the confines of the Western sexual paradigm. Roxane is a subject, but she is a subject absolutely *à part;* she appears as the Other not only because she is Persian and not Parisian, but also because she expresses her desire. Her exoticism results from this expression and costs her her existence as well. Indeed, the fates of Roxane, Julie, La Présidente de Tourvel, and Mme de Merteuil prove how the gesture of *unveil-*

ing, whether voluntary or involuntary, leads inexorably to death. Nancy K. Miller confirms that in most male-authored epistolary narratives of the eighteenth century, "the heroine's ultimate fate correlates directly with her performance in the sexual arena ... [and] illicit sex ... must be punished, preferably by death" (39).

The death of the woman who dared to desire, moreover, may be read as a symbolic projection of the (male) subject's fear before the knowledge of his own *aphanisis*, or fading. Elisabeth Bronfen, building on the work of Lacan, puts it in similar terms:

> Woman, in her split representation, is construed as a symptom for the split in the self, a symptom of death's presence, precisely because she is the site where the repressed anxiety about death re-emerges in a displaced, disfigured form ... Woman is ... closer to the real lack traced by mortality, even as she is also the symptom by which masculine culture can displace or repress this truth. (214-15, 217)

This insightful interpretation of woman-as-*symptom* does much to elucidate the so-called female destiny of the eighteenth-century heroine. Mme de Merteuil, for instance, *incarnates* Bronfen's notion that in woman, "anxiety about death ... re-emerges in a displaced, disfigured form": the final epistle of Laclos's text reveals that Merteuil "[est en vie] ... mais affreusement défigurée ... elle a particulièrement perdu un oeil" (378). When woman refuses to veil her body and her desire, she in effect transgresses the *arrangement* wherein she allows the male subject to deny what Lacan calls "[le] manque antécédent" caused by the (un)certainty of his own disappearance (194). The veil therefore constitutes a visual emblem of a crucial displacement whereby the strange desire to be assured of one's own aphanisis, or disappearance, is not replied to directly (Lacan 195); rather, it is redirected into longing for the Other.

The veil covers a referent–the female body–that is all too present and at the same time reveals that body for what it is, namely the origin of an existence whose end is as inevitable as it is unknowable. This semi-transparent, filmy object–defined in Larousse as *une étoffe qui protège*–mediates in order to protect the male subject from the truth of (non)-existence that is visibly inscribed in the field of Other. It is the silver shield of Perseus, screening the mortal from Medusa's gaze.

Mediating Desire

In Rousseau's *Julie* and in Riccoboni's *Lettres de Fanni Butlerd*, the veil may be read as an emblem of mediation between self and other. Within the epistolary economy, it mediates the subject-object relation by mitigating its truth, which according to Lacan is constituted by the superimposition of two lacks: alienation and separation. In the Lacanian vocabulary, alienation refers to the original loss suffered by the subject during the process of entry into language. In order to enter the realm of the Symbolic, the subject must shut the door to the Imaginary:

> lorsque le sujet apparaît quelque part comme sens, ailleurs il se manifeste comme *fading*, comme disparition ... il n'y a de sugissement du sujet au niveau du sens que de son *aphanisis* en l'Autre lieu, qui est celui de l'inconscient.... (Lacan 199, 201)

The emergence of symbolic meaning, Lacan insists, entails a disappearance from the realm of unconscious being and creates a space within the subject that is split-off but sensed nevertheless. The subject's shadowy *awareness* of that first fading, furthermore, creates a sense of alienation within the self.

According to Lacan, the alienation that the subject suffers—the feeling that the first image has been lost and cannot be found—is redirected into desire for the Other. Because the desire for the Other is an impossible attempt to veil the truth of human fading, it emerges as a confirmation of separation:

> le sujet ... apporte la réponse du manque antécédent, de sa propre disparition, qu'il vient situer ici au point du manque aperçu dans l'Autre ...[u]*n manque recouvre l'autre.* (Lacan 194-95, my emphasis)

With Rousseau and with Riccoboni, the written word and the veil negotiate the acknowledgment of lack in order to make it bearable. The interruptions, hesitations, and gaps that occur in spoken language, for example, testify to the opacity of communication. In contrast, writing smooths over the broken patterns of speech and creates an illusion of clarity and contact. The veil operates in much the same way with regard to visual communication; it allows the subject *not to see* the truth of sexual difference and division. By mediating desire, the veil cultivates ambiguity with respect to *le voir* and therefore blocks the knowledge of lack. The subject (here, Saint-Preux, Julie, and Fanni) depends upon this ambiguity, as I shall demonstrate; without it, desire can no longer be deferred and so the subject can no longer cover the truth of his or her own fading.

The verb *to mediate* comes to us from the Latin *mediare*–"to divide in the middle." Current-day usage–"to reconcile, to be the medium for settling differences"–therefore reflects a kind of etymological *about-face*. The verb that originally signified division has come to mean (re)union. This ambivalent term illustrates the equivocal function of the letter and the veil; both serve to join but also to divide writer from reader and the gaze from its object. Because the letter confirms a separation even as it professes to overcome it, and because the veil functions ultimately to *conceal presence*, these objects cultivate ambiguity.

Both letter and veil encode different paradoxes, yet their functions within the epistolary dialectic are analogous–both are symbolic go-betweens. The letter depends upon separation in time and space in order to suggest presence while the veil obviates the very presence upon which it depends. With the letter, the referent–the sender to whom the *je* refers–is altogether absent and the letter serves to re-presence him or her metonymically. With the veil, the referent–the body-object of a gaze–is *too present*; the veil strives to conceal a (female) body that is too much *there*. (It is paradoxical that what is *too much there*, too present, is the female's so-called lack as perceived by the male gaze.) In addition, the letter mediates desire in the absence of the gaze whereas the veil intervenes between subject and object when there are no words. Here the etymological ambivalence of the verb may be recalled, since these intermediary objects both divide and unite subject and object.

Within the epistolary exchange, the letter and the veil mediate desire by denying an avowal of difference; as such, they are emblems of *différance*. As intermediaries between subject and object, they illustrate Lacan's theory of the dialectic of desire. The metonymical displacements that govern this dialectic, he suggests, render it phantasmic: "la dialectique des objets du désir, en tant qu'elle fait le joint du désir du sujet au désir de l'Autre ... cette dialectique passe par ceci, qu'il n'y est pas répondu directement"

(195). The veil has everything to do with the displacement that characterizes desire, for it places in the space of the reciprocal gaze a kind of transparent obstacle. The subject's desire, moreover, *cannot* be directly faced–nor should it be–since the desire for the Other is ultimately the desire for one's own effacement.[2] The desire to know–to be assured of–one's eventual disappearance redirects itself onto the object, masquerading as love.

In Rousseau's *Nouvelle Héloïse* and in Riccoboni's *Fanni Butlerd*, the veil figures as an object of mediation between subject and object. In each of these texts, veil imagery manifests itself in two ways. As a concrete, physical object, it covers the beloved body (Julie) or a *representation* of that body (the portraits of Julie and Alfred). In this sense it creates a sort of *effet de présence* that is cultivated by the desiring subject for its own sake. As an *abstraction*, however, *le voile de l'illusion* becomes a figure for love's deceptions and desire's demise. Both authors reveal veiling to be the strategy that allows the subject (Julie and Fanni) to deny the failure of desire; however, I observe a contrast concerning the outcome of this symbolic veiling. In *La Nouvelle Héloïse*, the veil that Julie proffers hides the truth of desire that Rousseau names *le déchirement*. Even in death, the veil remains; the reader learns that "nulle main ne peut l'écarter" (Book V, Letter 9, 466). In contrast, Riccoboni depicts a female subject who first adopts *le voile de l'illusion* but then *removes* it and faces the void that the veil was meant to fill. The gesture of unveiling, or *dévoilement*, leads Fanni away from death and toward self-knowledge and life.

LE VOILE EST DÉCHIRÉ–JULIE, OU LA NOUVELLE HÉLOÏSE

The significance of the veil in Rousseau's novel has been debated at great length. Jean Starobinski interprets it as one of several obstacles barring the ideal of transparency:

---

[2] For Lacan, desire for the Other is nothing more than a transposition or redirection of the death drive:
> Le fantasme de sa mort, de sa disparition, est le premier objet que le sujet a à mettre en jeu dans cette dialectique [celle de l'aliénation et de la séparation], et il le met en effet–nous le savons par mille faits, ne serait-ce que par l'anorexie mentale. Nous savons aussi que le fantasme de sa mort est agité communément par l'enfant, dans ses rapports d'amour avec ses parents. (195)

> Rousseau désire la communication et la transparence des coeurs, mais il est frustré dans son attente et, choisissant la voie contraire, il accepte—et suscite—l'obstacle, qui lui permet de se replier dans la résignation passive et dans la certitude de son innocence. (*Transparence* 10)

Starobinski demonstrates that Saint-Preux and Julie place between themselves the very obstacles that impede their union. Because transparency is ultimately an impossibility, he writes, "il faut vivre dans l'opacité" (21). Several other critics have built upon Starobinski's scholarship in their efforts to decipher its meaning. Paul Pelckmans interprets Saint-Preux's dream of the veil, for example, as the supreme illustration of "[la] distance infranchissable ... [qui serait elle-même l'illustration de] la nouvelle opacité des rapports humains qui caractérisent les Lumières" (97). Anne Deneys-Tunney, in addition, proposes a schema wherein the veil, as it functions in Saint-Preux's dream and in Julie's death, "révèle qu'en Julie c'est la mère que désire Saint-Preux" (208):

> Le voile joue un rôle ambigu dans ce rêve ... [il] protège à la fois de l'identification brutale, ou de la conscience du désir d'inceste ... en même temps et surtout il protège de la réalisation de l'inceste; il est le 'voile impénétrable' qui ménage la virginité de Julie (on peut penser que 'le voile impénétrable' désigne l'hymen). (208)

This last interpretation seems to me problematic because Saint-Preux's dream of idealized (and thus unrealized) union comes *after* the lovers have experienced physical union; it is a song of experience and not a song of innocence. The substitution "par laquelle Julie devient symboliquement la mère" (208) is illustrated in the text; however, it is not clear that in replacing her own mother in the dream, Julie becomes *Saint-Preux's* mother. In fact, Saint-Preux appears not to have any kin, whereas Julie's parents dictate her actions absolutely and are in turn affected by them. The symbolic replacement announces (in my view) the transfer in Julie's roles from that of daughter to that of wife and mother; Mme d'Etanges tells her daughter "[m]on enfant ... il faut remplir son sort ... [t]u seras mère à ton tour" (Book V, Letter 9, 466). One might rebut that it is precisely Saint-Preux's lack of familial ties that supports an Oedipal reading of the dream, that because he has no mother, "son désir pour Julie est en fait un désir d'inceste" (Deneys-Tunney 210). Still, such a reading seems not to take into account one of the greater paradoxes of the text; the fact that the symbolic *voilement* is a response to an all-too literal *déchirement*.

If the *chevalier's* dream speaks of a longing to "toucher le voile [et ainsi] de réaliser l'inceste" (Deneys-Tunney 209), it must be remembered that the dream of reconciliation, of which the veil is the emblem, is a response to the "crisis" of physical possession. The dream of *voilement* is a response to a profanation that has already occurred rather than an expression of anticipation. Rousseau makes it quite clear, furthermore, that while the members of the *petite société*–including Julie herself–seek to deny the fact that Julie is both flawed and mortal, the extradiegetic reader cannot enter into that society and must instead recognize that *le voile est déchiré*.

Julie's bodily conduct is as important as her exemplary moral behavior. Indeed, one may regard her renunciation as a response to the so-called excess of her physical desires. Despite her appearance of modesty, it is *Julie* who avows her attraction and acts upon it by initiating both the *baiser du bosquet* and the lovemaking with Saint-Preux:

> Il faut donc l'avouer enfin, ce fatal secret trop mal déguisé! ... [j]e n'ai rien négligé pour arrêter le progrès de cette passion funeste ... je t'adore en dépit de moi-même. (Julie to Saint-Preux, Book I, Letter 4, 15)

> J'ai interrompu ma lettre pour m'aller promener dans des bocages qui sont près de notre maison ... [j]e choisissais les lieux que nous devons parcourir ensemble .. [p]armi les bosquets naturels que forme ce lieu charmant, il en est un plus charmant que les autres, dans lequel je me plais davantage, et où, par cette raison, je destine une petite surprise à mon ami. (Julie to Saint-Preux, Book I, Letter 13, 33)

> [J]e me sens une hardiesse que je n'eus jamais; et, si tu l'oses partager, ce soir, ce soir même peut acquitter mes promesses, et payer d'une seule fois toutes les dettes de l'amour ...[v]iens cette après-midi chez ma Fanchon, je t'expliquerai le reste et te donnerai les instructions nécessaires.... (Julie to Saint-Preux, Book I, Letter 53, 95-96)

Rousseau evokes the physical experiences of his protagonist–sex, pregnancy, miscarriage, death–rather than depicting them explicitly. In keeping with the esthetic of the veil, that which is hidden is most weighty with significance. The symbolic veiling of Julie's body (by both intradiegetic and extradiegetic readers) belies a desire to conceal the meaning it conveys to the community assembled at Clarens. This meaning is the knowledge of division that originates in the experience of sexual difference.

Julie herself draws a veil over this knowledge in order to protect her idyllic community. In Books II and III this community finds itself reconfigured as Julie sacrifices *amour* in the name of *devoir*. As she gradually capitulates to her father's wishes and to Claire's admonition that she obey them, Julie discovers that she can no longer offer her body to her lover. Instead, she sends him a painted likeness of herself. The portrait becomes a stand-in for physical presence, and representation allows for repetition. Letter 22, authored by Saint-Preux and sent to Julie, records a scene of repetition wherein the *déchirement* of union–the source of loss–is again performed:

> Je tenais donc ce paquet avec une inquiète curiosité dont je n'étais pas le maître; je m'efforçais de palper à travers les enveloppes ce qu'il pouvait contenir ... j'ai senti palpiter mon coeur à chaque papier que j'ôtais, et je me suis bientôt trouvé tellement oppressé que j'ai été forcé de respirer un moment sur la dernière enveloppe ... Julie! ... ô ma Julie! *le voile est déchiré* ... je te vois ... Dieux! quels tourments de flammes mes avides regards puisent dans cet objet inattendu! ô comme il ranime au fond de mon coeur tous les mouvements impétueux que ta présence y faisait naître! (200-01, my emphasis)

Here, the portrait acts as an intermediary between subject and object, and the paper wrappings that cover Julie's likeness function like a veil. The act of unwrapping the portrait reactivates Saint-Preux's memory of presence as well as the separation brought about by the pain of union.

In *La Nouvelle Héloïse*, *déchirement* signifies the division that has its origins in the ordeal of physical union. The subsequent *voilement* strives to remedy this *mal* by rendering the beloved body inaccessible. The veil therefore mediates between the opacity of experience and the transparency that is held out as an ideal. In keeping with the paradoxes that inform this esthetic of *distancing*, it is Julie–who formerly eradicated all distance and seduced Saint-Preux–who proffers the veil. In response to Saint-Preux's declarations that "le voile est déchiré" (Letters 22, 200 and 6, 232) she exhorts him to cover over this truth:

> On s'égare un seul moment de la vie, on se détourne d'un seul pas de la droite route; aussitôt une pente inévitable nous entraîne et nous perd; on tombe enfin dans le gouffre, et l'on se réveille épouvanté de se trouver couvert de crimes avec un coeur né pour la vertu. Mon bon ami, *laissons retomber ce voile*: avons-nous besoin de voir le précipice affreux qu'il nous cache pour éviter d'en approcher? (Book III, Letter 18, 260, my emphasis)

Julie's long process of *voilement* is a response to the experience of *déchirement*. The veils that she places between herself and her former lover include physical separation and an appearance of *bonheur*. So effective are these illusions, Wolmar writes to Claire, that "[u]n voile de sagesse et d'honnêteté fait tant de replis autour de son coeur qu'il n'est plus possible à l'oeil humain d'y pénétrer, pas même au sien propre" (Book IV, Letter 13, 382).

Swan Song

The gesture of veiling brings life, where the *déchirement* of physical contact brought only death. Julie's renunciation may be read as an act of self-preservation even though, as she ultimately confesses, her sober life is just one step removed from death: "vivre sans peine n'est pas un état d'homme; vivre ainsi c'est être mort ... [j]e ne vois partout que sujets de contentement, et je ne suis pas contente; une langueur secrète s'insinue au fond de mon coeur; je le sens vide et gonflé ... je suis trop heureuse; le bonheur m'ennuie" (Book VI, Letter 8, 528). In a footnote to this letter, Rousseau admonishes his protagonist for her contradictions and tells his readers that it is her "chant de cygne" (528). Transparency has become its own obstacle, and the frail illusion of happiness no longer holds. The gesture of veiling has enabled Julie to survive her *previous* deaths, to which she alludes in her final letter: "[a]près tant de sacrifices, je compte pour peu celui qui me reste à faire: ce n'est que mourir une fois de plus" (565). I ascertain that these earlier, symbolic deaths include the swoon in the *bosquet*, the fall inflicted upon her by her father's rage, and the "fatal" union with Saint-Preux.

The gesture of veiling gave Julie life yet could not be sustained; deep within her heart–whose surface, Wolmar tells us, is clouded with folds of veils–languishes "le premier sentiment qui [l']a fait vivre" (564). This "first feeling"–her desire for Saint-Preux–re-emerges at the moment of death: "il me ranime quand je me meurs" (564). The illusion that enabled her to veil her unhappiness–and therefore survive–cannot ultimately conquer the lack that it is meant to conceal. This lack, Anne Deneys-Tunney explains, has its origins in "la découverte d'une fêlure au coeur du désir" (198). The veil's mediating gesture fails: "[j]e me suis longtemps fait illusion. Cette illusion me fut salutaire; elle se détruit au moment où je n'en ai plus besoin" (564). Its failure articulates the triumph of *différence* over *différance*.

This failure, moreover, is staged by Julie as a kind of *bel échec* through the topos that Elisabeth Bronfen calls the beautiful death. Julie stages her own death just as she staged her life; both may be seen as *mises en scène* or *performances* of transparency. Bronfen concurs that

> [Julie] borrows authority from death ... she 'writes' a beautiful death with her body in two separate registers. She 'authors' a united family and she creates that death, which draws her friends and the readers into the text's composition ... [a]s its dying centre, Julie is also the text's self-reflexive moment, by commenting on the end or decomposition that always informs textual production ... [i]t is a superlatively poetical death, because it fulfills the 'text' of her good life before it can move into a decline. (80-81)

Julie's body is a text of flesh that invites its readers to consider the illusion of the sign's transparency even as they face the reality of its decomposition. It is evident that the intradiegetic readers of this text–Claire, Wolmar, the servants, and to a lesser extent Saint-Preux–choose not to see its decomposition and instead cover the referent with a piece of fabric so transparent that it reveals what it purports to conceal. The esthetic of veiling reaches its apotheosis with the death of *l'inconcevable Julie*. The knowledge of division that Julie covered over in life, which originated in the experience of physical union, is now unveiled and desire shows itself for what it is, namely a symptom of that earlier lack that Lacan calls *fading*. In *La Nouvelle Héloïse*, the experience of death restores being and thus eradicates fading where that of desire brought only a vain search for completion.

The veil that previously protected the subject by deferring the avowal of sexual difference now intervenes to shield the survivors from the knowledge of Julie's death. As an object of mediation between life and death, the veil that shrouds Julie's visage illustrates one way "in which the gap death produces can be denied or mitigated, in which the absent body can be re-presenced" (Bronfen 83). That Julie's *survivors*–most notably, her servants and Claire–assume the role of veiling supports an interpretation wherein the *voile de l'illusion* prolongs life while its *déchirement* figures real or symbolic death. Letter 11 of Book VI recounts how Claire transforms herself into the purveyor of illusion by covering the all-too-mortal face of *la divine Julie* with the veil that Saint-Preux brought back from his travels:

> [A]près plus de trente-six heures, par l'extrême chaleur qu'il faisait, les chairs commençaient à se corrompre; et quoique le visage eût gardé ses traits et sa douceur, on y voyait déjà quelques signes d'altération. Je le dis à Mme d'Orbe …[e]lle m'entendit et, prenant son parti sans rien dire, elle sortit de la chambre. Je la vis rentrer un moment après, tenant un voile d'or brodé de perles que vous lui aviez apporté des Indes. Puis, s'approchant du lit, elle baisa le voile, en couvrit en pleurant la face de son amie, et s'écria d'une voix éclatante: 'Maudite soit l'indigne main qui verra ce visage défiguré!' … Elle a fait tant d'impression sur tous nos gens et sur tout le peuple, que la défunte ayant été mise au cercueil dans ses habits et avec les plus grandes précautions, elle a été portée et inhumée dans cet état, sans qu'il soit trouvé personne assez hardi pour toucher au voile. (561-62)

In a philosophical footnote to this letter, Rousseau takes care to point out that Saint-Preux's dream is the source both for Julie's death and for Claire's gesture of denial: "l'événement n'est pas prédit parce qu'il arrivera; mais il arrive parce qu'il a été prédit" (562). Julie's body signifies the original source of lack–the knowledge of life's fading. The gold veil that covers it is a sign meant to distance this spectral referent and to occult its truth.

Death represents an absolute *déchirement* and therefore is most strenuously denied. In the final letters of *La Nouvelle Héloïse*, the *event* of death is presented as the fruit of a kiss and was contained *en germe* in the first instance of bliss. The lovers's first contact–the "mortal kiss" in a shaded wood–tore a veil and introduced irrevocable division where before there was the promise of union. The transparency of the original promise–of *l'attente*–cannot be recuperated, but the trauma can be denied for a time. Through the gesture of veiling, a false transparency may be sustained and happiness performed, if not truly experienced. The final moment of separation by death is embraced as an artful fruition of earlier deaths. While Julie willingly abandons the illusion of transparency in order to embrace the opacity that knows no obstacles, her survivors veil her body in order to cover over death's truth. If the gesture of veiling in Rousseau's text represents a denial of original division, it is a gesture that succeeds for everyone but Julie.

Fanni Butlerd–le dévoilement

If Rousseau invents the gesture of veiling as a symbolic way to deny a knowledge of division that is deemed intolerable, one may observe in Riccoboni's *Lettres de Mistress Fanni Butlerd* a different outcome regarding the veil. Both texts may be said to depict the failure of an ideal: total transparency with the Other. However, although both Julie and Fanni confront the same obstacle–lack of transparency–they respond very differently. Julie blinds herself to her unhappiness and ultimately chooses death whereas Riccoboni's protagonist undergoes a process of *enlightenment* that, while painful, assures her survival. In contrast to Julie, who strove in vain to live life "sans peine," Fanni finds herself "éclairé[e] par [s]es peines" (Letter 116, 182). This *éclaircissement* of which Fanni speaks in her final letter may be read as a kind of life-affirming *dévoilement*.

The symbolic movement from *voilement* to *dévoilement* in *Fanni Butlerd* contrasts completely with Rousseau's movement from *déchirement* to *voilement*. Because the desire for the Other is always in some sense a longing to get beyond or outside of one's self, it veils the process of reflection that leads to self-knowledge; in Riccoboni's text, this process is described as a *descente en soi-même* (Letters 114 and 116). Whereas Julie cuts herself off from this process—we may recall Wolmar's image of her heart obscured by veils—Fanni is one of "ceux qui ... ont continuellement besoin de descendre en eux-mêmes [afin d'entendre] ... le témoignage de leur coeur" (Letter 114, 178). Only when transparency is acknowledged as an *ideal*, Riccoboni suggests, and not tested against the real, can one survive the loss of the Other without sacrificing one's self.

La Nouvelle Héloïse depicts the torn truth of presence very early on and, as Deneys-Tunney points out, "[l]a suite du roman ne sera qu'une gestion du traumatisme initial du baiser" (206). In contrast to Rousseau's text, which opens with the afflicted Saint-Preux's "il faut vous fuir, mademoiselle" and therefore emphasizes separation, Riccoboni's text opens by alluding to a dream of union:

> PREMIÈRE LETTRE
> *Jeudi à midi*
>
> Après avoir bien réfléchi sur votre songe, je vous félicite, Mylord, de cette vivacité d'imagination qui vous fait rêver de si jolies choses; ménagez ce bien; une douce erreur forme tout l'agrément de notre vie. Heureux par de riantes illusions, qu'a-t-on besoin de la réalité? Loin de remplir l'idée que nous avions d'elle, souvent elle détruit le bonheur dont nous jouissons. Livrez-vous au plaisir de rêver, et sachez-moi gré de je ne sais quel mouvement qui me force à m'intéresser à tout ce qui vous touche. Je n'ai point dormi, point rêvé; mais tant songé, tant pensé, que je ne crois plus penser. Adieu, Mylord. (Letter 1, 5-6)

Although the content of Alfred's dream is not explicit, one may infer that it conveys images of physical union. In this initial letter I observe a kind of philosophy of desire that will inform Fanni's entire correspondence: the dream of transparency with the Other is an ideal that is recognized and celebrated as a wonderful impossibility. For Riccoboni, the ideal must not be tested against the real; in Fanni's words, it is "une douce erreur," "un bien," "[une] riante illusion." The relation between self and other, moreover, is presented from the beginning of the correspondence as a construction that is *imaginary*; Fanni congratulates Alfred on the "vivacité d'imagination" that fed his vision.

Unlike Julie, who invents the strategy of veiling in order to occult the broken truth of desire, Fanni faces the fact of failed transparency. While her images of ideal union are often fanciful (she dreams for instance of visiting Alfred as a fairy and of watching him unseen thanks to a magic ring), she recognizes that her dreams are an escape from reality and nothing more. Her relationship with Alfred, as she herself writes, is both flawed and finite: Alfred stays away, and love fades. It is worth noting that Fanni confronts this reality very early on in the correspondence, even before she is united with her *amant*:

> ... quels seront vos remords, *quand la froideur succédant à la tendresse*, vous serez forcé de vous dire: *J'ai détruit la félicité d'une femme digne de mon estime ... j'ai porté la douleur dans le sein de celle dont les innocentes pensées assuraient la joie.* (Letter 7, 11, my emphasis)

> Hélas, ces jours heureux passent avec une rapidité; ils me conduisent à celui qui va me priver de vous, m'enlever mon bien le plus cher. (Letter 37, 51)

> Quand mon cher Alfred ne m'aimera plus ... je me ferai catholique, et j'irai habiter dans cette maison paisible [le couvent]. (Letter 51, 71)

The knowledge that Fanni faces is the same knowledge that Julie and Saint-Preux find to be utterly intolerable: "la félicité," she writes, "n'est point dans les objets où on la cherche" (Letter 75, 115).

Although she does love Alfred (Letters 6 and 7 record her eager avowal), she does not allow her sense of self to be subsumed by the desire for the Other. In effect, her affectionate taunts to her lover reveal a deep effort to preserve a sense of self:

> Vous dérangez tous mes projets, vous détruisez le plan du reste de ma vie.... (Letter 4, 7)

> Avant que vous me fissiez éprouver ces mouvements auxquels vous voulez que mon ame [sic] s'abandonne, j'étois tranquille, contente, je n'avais de peines que celles dont aucun être ne peut s'affranchir, et que nous devons tous supporter dans la position

> où le sort nous a placés; vous m'arrachez à cet état. Semblable à Pigmalion, vous animez un marbre; craignez qu'il ne vous reproche un jour de l'avoir tiré de sa paisible insensibilité. (Letter 7, 11)

Whereas Rousseau's protagonists fear the loss of the Other, Riccoboni's fear the loss of the self. Her protagonists (I am thinking of Juliette Catesby as well as of Fanni) insist upon preserving the sense of self before they can give themselves over to the *douce erreur* of desire. In *Lettres de Mistress Fanni Butlerd*, this integrity or wholeness of the self is described as an inner tranquillity or peace.

LE VOILE DE L'ILLUSION

For Fanni, the ideal presence attained in image and word is an illusion that is favored over actual presence. Here it is important to emphasize that the idealized depictions of the absent lover are recognized as such. Fanni is quite conscious of her *erreur*, and while she indeed gives her thoughts over to fantasy, she never loses sight of the fact that love casts a veil over the real:

> Sexe dangereux! c'est bien vous qui possédez l'art de séduire ... [c]'est votre ame que vous parez ... [u]ne ombre favorable fait sortir à nos yeux mille couleurs brillantes, et nous cache une partie du sujet varié qui s'offre à notre contemplation.... (Letter 5, 8-9)

It is not hard to grasp Riccoboni's feminism in this letter, for her protagonist draws a dividing line between men (*vous*) and women (*nous*). The reader finds him or herself necessarily on the side of a female perspective. Further in this letter Fanni employs the metaphor of the thorny bloom to illustrate her view that love's pleasure masks a hidden pain: "pense-t-on en les voyant [les fleurs], aux épines dont la plus belle est environnée?" (9).

If Fanni breathes deep of the bloom, she never forgets the thorn. For though she indulges in visions of union with Alfred, she fears the loss of self that that union requires. Letter 27 records the troubled thoughts of a young woman who knows that in idealizing the Other she risks losing a part of herself:

> Aimer, s'attacher, quelle folie! ... [c]es jardins si beaux, où je me promenais hier, ne m'ont présenté que votre idée; je cherchois vos traits sur ces marbres que l'art a rendus presque parlans ... mon cher Alfred, ces premiers jours du printems animent les passions ... cette admirable harmonie ... éveille en nous un désir indéterminé, et nous avertit de chercher un bien qui nous manque. Ah ce bien est l'amour! ... [h]élas, ce bien, je l'ai trouvé! pourquoi ne puis-je oublier qu'il est souvent la source des peines les plus amères? Je vois ici un triste exemple des effets de la complaisance. Que j'en suis effrayée! Je me croyais si sûre de ma fierté, de mon indifférence, que j'ai fait mille imprécations contre moi, que j'ai prié le ciel de me punir, si jamais j'étois assez foible pour préférer le bonheur d'un amant à mes principes, à ma tranquillité. (37)

Throughout the correspondence, Fanni balances the pleasure of loving the Other with its price. Unlike Rousseau's protagonist, who regards self-sacrifice as a virtue, she calculates its price and ascertains that it is too high.

The sacrifice of living for and in another, Riccoboni suggests, is bound to fail because difference can never fully be veiled. Transparency may be enjoyed in dreams and in visions but it can never truly be lived. In Chapter Four I pointed out that Fanni's *substitutions* of presence prepare her for the reality of love's dissolution. When Alfred finally admits to his act of betrayal and informs Fanni of his betrothal to a wealthier woman, Fanni is wounded but she is not surprised. She foresaw the infidelity from the beginning of the correspondence and therefore maintained a protective self-scrutiny in anticipation of the loss: "[j]'ai fait bien des découvertes dans mon coeur, depuis que je vous l'ai donné" (Letter 80, 125). Here we may recall the image of Julie's clouded heart in order to contrast Fanni's self-awareness with that character's loss of self.

Fanni's refusal to veil the experience of difference leads her toward life where Julie's strenuous veiling results in death. Alfred abandons her, but she never abandons herself; moreover, she is constant while Alfred is not what he appeared to be:

> Vous n'êtes point celui que j'aimois, non, vous ne l'êtes point; vous ne l'avez jamais été ... [v]ous ne pouvez douter que je ne vous aye tendrement aimé; soyez sûr que je vous aime encore: mais de nouvelles découvertes, le tems, l'événement qui m'en-

> gage à faire une démarche si contraire à mes sentiments, votre absence, les réflexions qui se présentent si naturellement à l'esprit par la vue du présent, et le souvenir du passé, me rendront peut-être à moi-même, et me procureront une paix que je ne pourrais trouver dans l'avilissement d'une passion dont je ne sentirais plus que les peines. (Letter 114, 177-79)

For Riccoboni, women live, love, and suffer differently from men: "vous n'aimez pas comme nous" (Letter 97, 156). Because of this, difference can be deferred but not denied. Men, she continues, require women to be the purveyors of illusion, and women must decide whether or not to perform this role.

Fanni refuses to veil herself in order to attain the Other. When Alfred offers to keep her as his mistress after announcing his intended marriage to another woman, Fanni articulates her outrage by evoking images of the veil:

> vous voyez tomber le voile de l'illusion; vous vous efforcez de le rattacher sur mes yeux. Ingrat, oubliez-vous que votre main l'a cruellement déchiré? Non, je ne vois plus en vous celui que je me plaisois à chérir. (Letter 108, 170)

In a pattern that reverses the order in Rousseau's text, Fanni moves from a state of *voilement* to one of *dévoilement*. By giving up love's illusion she strives to recuperate the peace and tranquillity that she had lost: "[t]ranquille dans mon obscurité, j'éloignois de moi tout ce qui pouvait troubler une vie, sinon heureuse, au moins paisible. Pourquoi votre art perfide sut-il me voiler vos desseins?" (Letter 116, 185).

Two Hearts

In each of the texts that I have discussed, veiling emerges as a mediating strategy that sustains the illusion of transparency between self and other. This strategy depends upon the occultation of the female body and of the mortal reality it proclaims. The contrast that I have observed between *voilement* (in Rousseau) and *dévoilement* (in Riccoboni) manifests itself clearly at the end of each text. In both, the female protagonist composes a final letter in which she evokes an image of her heart. In Letter 12 of Book VI, Julie describes the negative revelation that accompanies the moment of death:

> j'eus beau vouloir étouffer le premier sentiment qui m'a fait vivre, il s'est concentré dans mon coeur. Il s'y réveille au moment qu'il n'est plus à craindre; il me soutient quand mes forces m'abandonnent; il me ranime quand je me meurs ... [h]élas! j'achève de vivre comme j'ai commencé. J'en dis trop peut-être en ce moment où le coeur ne déguise plus rien.... (564, 566)

In this passage Julie finally looks within and faces both her desire and her failure to recognize it as her own. In contradiction to Wolmar's assertion that no human gaze–including that of Julie–can "penetrate" the veils that shroud her heart, this young lover casts aside the illusion that simultaneously prolonged her life and brought about its end.

Fanni's final letter (116) expresses a kind of personal renaissance and therefore contrasts with Julie's swan song. In it she admonishes Alfred for his cruel treatment of her and reacts to his offer of friendship with expressions of moral outrage:

> Tremblez, ingrat; je vais porter une main hardie jusqu'au fond de votre coeur, en développer tous les replis secrets, la perfidie, et détaillant l'horrible trahison....
> ... L'idée fantastique qui faisoit mon bonheur, s'est évanouie pour jamais; cette idole chérie, adorée, dénuée des ornemens dont mon imagination l'avait embellie, ne m'offre plus qu'une esquisse imparfaite ... [a]insi mon coeur, trompé par ses désirs, éclairé par ses peines, n'a joui que d'une vaine erreur. Il la regrette peut-être, mais il ne peut la recouvrer. Adieu, Mylord.... (183, 191)

Fanni's final letter shows an evolution from idealization to realization; in it, she embraces life and articulates her experience in her own terms. This female subject expresses a kind of *éclaircissement* that contrasts completely with Julie's *obscurcissement*. She achieves self-knowledge by refusing to sacrifice herself for the Other and by recognizing in love an illusion that is not only *salutaire*–Julie's adjective–but also *néfaste*.

In Rousseau's text, the veil shields the (male) gaze from an object that proclaims the certainty of difference and death–the female body. As such, it is the preeminent metaphor for what Elisabeth Bronfen calls the "narcissistic protection against death's presence in life" (217). In Riccoboni's text, the female subject accepts the veil but then rejects it, preferring the clear pangs of solitude to the cloudy happiness of union. Whereas Rousseau ultimately identifies Woman to be the vehicle "by which masculine culture can repress or displace the truth [of mortality]," Riccoboni refuses such an identification by suggesting that it is an untenable construction (Bronfen 217). She does this in a subtle manner, by contrasting Alfred's worldly ambition with Fanni's inner world of contemplation. Alfred's act of infidelity reveals him to be seeking out external signs of privilege and worth, and Fanni unmasks the futility of this gesture in Letter 114:

> [ê]tre heureux dans l'opinion des autres; sacrifier tout au plaisir fastueux d'attirer des regards; briller d'un éclat étranger qui n'est point en nous, et n'est un bien que parce que la foule en est privée; c'est sans doute pour ceux que le hasard a placés dans un jour avantageux.... (178)

Alfred leaves Fanni for a woman of higher means, and in so doing he betrays not only her but also himself: Fanni includes him among those who seek "un dédommagement des vertus qu'ils n'ont pas, des qualités qu'ils négligent, du bonheur après lequel ils courent en vain, du dégoût et de l'ennui qui les suit et les dévore" (178).

In contrast to Rousseau, Riccoboni exposes the failure of the subject-object relation by suggesting that the possessive quest for the Other leads only to a loss of self; it is a vain search for a completeness that does not exist. In Lacanian terms, Alfred's desire and its displacement from Fanni to the nameless noblewoman serves only to recall his own fading–the qualities that he lacks, the happiness that will surely escape him, and the sense of emptiness or futility that "devours" his existence. Fanni herself alludes to the kind of symbolic death that can occur when one's desire for the Other obscures the process of self-reflection: "[j]e souhaite, Mylord, et je le souhaite sincèrement, que rien ne vous force à regretter la vie agréable et paisible à laquelle vous renoncez...." (178).

In *Lettres de Mistress Fanni Butlerd*, Riccoboni explores the subject-object relation and concludes that "la félicité n'est point dans les objets où on la cherche" (Letter 75, 115). Her protagonist refuses to sacrifice herself for a male illusion of integration: "[t]rop délicate pour vous partager ... je ne vous promets point de l'amitié" (Letter 114, 179). Instead, Fanni accepts the truth uncovered by Alfred's infidelity–"[v]ous n'êtes pas celui que j'aimois ..." (Letter 114, 177). She then composes a final letter (116) in which she urges her former lover to seek out a sense of wholeness *within* himself, as she has done, by reflecting deeply on the nature of his being: "[d]escendez en vous-même, Mylord, osez vous interroger, vous répondre...." (183). This *interior* dialogue within the self, Riccoboni suggests, leads the (female) subject away from error and loss toward a new wisdom based on acceptance: "mon coeur, trompé par ses désirs, éclairé par ses peines, n'a joui que d'une vaine erreur. Il la regrette peut-être, mais il ne peut la recouvrer" (191).

Postlude:

WINTER INTO SPRING

Persephone sat brooding in the cold hollows of the Underworld. From time to time she broke the stasis of that obscure palace by shifting her pale body beneath the dark garments she now wore. The god Hades was nowhere and everywhere, a blindness that moved in the night. The bride of Death was broken and forlorn, yet within her a new form of music was making itself heard—the music of pomegranates and gemstones and flickering flames. Persephone began to understand that the green leaves and light above could not exist without the shadows below. Until the moment when she knelt to pluck that colorful bloom, she had known only the upper regions of breezes and trees. Now, although cut off from the physical world, she had access to a dream realm of image and memory. She understood that in place of that sunlit narcissus—the object of her desire—she had acquired its *image*. That image, she knew, would never fade: in her mind she could reach eternally for its ideal touch, gaze forever at its painted surface.

In the myth of Persephone, the female body becomes the preeminent emblem for mortal transformation—described by Keats as "beauty that must die" ("Ode on Melancholy"). Sorrow and memory mark the myth, as Edith Hamilton points out:

> In the stories of both goddesses, Demeter and Persephone, the idea of sorrow was foremost. Demeter, goddess of the harvest wealth, was still more the divine sorrowing mother who saw her daughter die each year. Persephone was the radiant maiden of the spring and the summertime ... [yet she] knew how brief that beauty was; fruits, flowers, leaves, all the fair growth of the earth,

must end with the coming of the cold and pass like herself into
the power of death ... every spring ... she brought with her the
memory of where she had come from; with all her bright beauty
there was something strange and awesome about her. (63-64)

Memory figures prominently in the myth since it functions as the
vehicle for images: while she resides in Hades, Persephone imagines
the light above. And when, each year, she rushes forth from cold
darkness to return to her mother's embrace, she carries within her
the picture of her shadow home.

I have come to think of Persephone as an allegory for the
woman writer–"strange and awesome," she brings to the Light a
clear memory of opacity. Like Orpheus, the preeminent male poet
of myth, Persephone achieves an intimate knowledge of the unseen
realm and, returning to the world, communicates that knowledge.
Maurice Blanchot observes in the Orphic journey a primary tale depicting poetic creation:

> c'est vers Eurydice qu'Orphée est descendu: *Eurydice est, pour
> lui, l'extrême que l'art puisse atteindre, elle est, sous un nom qui la
> dissimule et sous un voile qui la couvre, le point profondément
> obscur vers lequel l'art, le désir, la mort, la nuit semblent tendre ...*
> Ce 'point,' [Eurydice], l'oeuvre d'Orphée ne consiste pas cependant à en assurer l'approche en descendant vers la profondeur.
> Son oeuvre, c'est de le ramener au jour et de lui donner, dans le
> jour, figure, forme, et réalité. (225, my emphasis)

Blanchot reads Orpheus's descent as a primary allegory for the
poet's work, yet his interpretation privileges a male paradigm of
creation insofar as Orpheus's return to light depends upon the
definitive veiling of the feminine. Indeed, Blanchot confirms that
beyond the Orphic descent, it is the *failure* of the quest that illustrates the predicament of (male) poetic creation: "Orphée peut
tout, sauf regarder ce 'point' [Eurydice] en face, sauf regarder le
centre de la nuit dans la nuit ... dans le mouvement de sa migration,
[il] oublie l'oeuvre qu'il doit accomplir, et il l'oublie nécessairement" (225-26).

Failure, Blanchot writes, defines the Orphic journey: I add that
Orpheus's failure emerges as a terrible recognition of impotence before the feminine. Moreover, the need to *deny* such impotence

drives the male creator to destroy that which reminds him of it, and so Eurydice falls back into a silent realm of shades. It is in this sense that I have read the deaths of Roxane, Madame de Merteuil, and Julie: in order for the male subject to bring form into being, he must *deform* the feminine. These "exquisite cadavers" may be seen as eighteenth-century evocations of Eurydice–veiled figures of obscurity and metonymies for death (Miller 37). Orpheus descends into a state of non-being in an attempt to recuperate that "center of night" that is the feminine; however, his backward glance ensures the failure of his quest. His error proves to be fatal for Eurydice but not (at first) for him; it shields him from impotence and allows him to return to the light alone.

In a very different sense, Persephone enters death's realm with no quest or object before her, and because of this, she cannot fail. In submitting to the darkness, she submits to her own death and therefore to her life. Her role in the myth may be dismissed as a passive one; however, by letting Night enter her she ultimately regains access to the Light. Her submission brings a rich reward–she is able to weave forever between life and death, repeating the story of death each year as she brings green shoots and pale blooms to the world above. It is in this way that I read Persephone as a figure for the female creator. The difference may be described in the following way: Orpheus gains a secondary *knowledge* of death while Persephone is transformed by the intimate *experience* of it. To have knowledge of death is not to feel it.

The monophonic epistolary texts that I have discussed consistently depict a female protagonist who learns to embrace life by drawing near to death. Graffigny's Peruvian princess is abducted by Spanish *conquistadores* whom she names "mes ravisseurs;" she begins her narrative by relating her experience of capture and speaks of existing in "un abîme d'obscurité" (Letter 1, 257). Later in the tale, Zilia again *feels death* and in that same moment draws on memory and image: "[r]eçois ... les derniers sentiments de mon coeur, il n'a reçu que ton image...." (Letter 6, 274). The princess passes through the underworld of loss and ultimately emerges whole–in giving up the Other, she regains herself. Similarly, Riccoboni's protagonist Fanni may be read as an eighteenth-century Persephone. The young Englishwoman who faces the knowledge that "la félicité ... n'est point dans les objets où on la cherche" recalls the Greek maiden who reaches for a flower only to have it recede forever from her grasp (Letter 75, 115). Fanni Butlerd finds herself transformed by loss and retreats to a dim realm of her own making. By the end of her narrative, however, the winter of mourning has passed and Fanni returns to life, her heart enlightened by pain.

These quiet heroines illustrate two themes of the myth that I have employed throughout my inquiry into the nature of Lyric during the French Enlightenment: mediation and recuperation. By reflecting on death, they achieve an understanding of life, and therefore mediate between self-destruction (Zilia and Fanni both contemplate suicide) and self-preservation. This kind of mediation, I have suggested, captures something of the elusive quality of eighteenth-century lyric since the threat of destruction ultimately transformed poetic form and therefore preserved it. In addition, Zilia and Fanni initially suffer a loss of self but then recuperate what they had lost. By choosing self-expression over self-effacement and autonomy over a state of dependence, they recover a sense of wholeness that had been taken from them. At the heart of the Enlightenment, epistolary poets like Graffigny and Riccoboni chose to depict the experience of opacity from a female perspective. By *opacity* I mean the absences and silences that form the reality of human experience and contrast with the ideal of transparency. Unlike the well-known narratives of Montesquieu, Rousseau, and Laclos, in which the death of the feminine sustains the illusion of transparency, female-authored narratives reconcile the imperfect real with the failed ideal.

The epistolary form evolved, as I and others have argued, in response to the socio-historical circumstances of the early Enlightenment, and mediated between the *Ancien Régime* and the modern age. During an era in which lyric poetry was being increasingly devalued in favor of philosophical and epistemological discourses, the letter emerged as the vehicle of lyricism. The reign of Louis XIV constituted a relative winter for lyricism as a result of an esthetic that mirrored the ideology of *absolutisme*. Under the pen of Malherbe and Boileau, the Lyric was ravished and relegated to the societal unconscious. The chiseled beauty of Racine's plays attests to this static *winter* of lyricism, yet it also reveals its permanence. With the Enlightenment, epistolary prose offered poets such as Graffigny and Rousseau a more mobile form in which to diffuse emotion and image.

Epistolary lyric cultivates an esthetic of evocation and suggestion. In letter-texts, as in poems, much is left unsaid and images stand in for actions. This emphasis on what is unseen or unknown is constitutive of the monophonic register and as such is eminently poetic. Like the poet, the *épistolière* does not truly anticipate a response, but rather writes out of a white space within. That white space of solitude manifests itself in letter-texts as blank space. Along with these blanks, which also influence the composition and reception of poems, letter-texts cultivate the esthetics of evocation through their relatively short length and their lack of closure. As such they lend themselves easily to the designation of *poésie en prose*. During the *Siècle des Lumières*, the figurative exploration of opacity took place in prose rather than in verse, and the lyric *je* recorded in letters the song of winter turning into spring.

BIBLIOGRAPHY

Allem, Maurice, ed. *Anthologie poétique française: XVI siècle.* Vol. 1. Paris: Flammarion, 1965.
Altman, Janet. *Epistolarity: Approaches to a Form.* Columbus: Ohio State UP, 1982.
Anderson, David L. "Abélard and Héloïse: eighteenth-century motif." *Studies on Voltaire and the Eighteenth Century* vol. 84 (1971): 7-51.
André, Arlette. "Le Féminisme chez Mme Riccoboni." *Studies on Voltaire and the Eighteenth Century* 193 (1980): 1988-95.
Balzac, Honoré de. *Le Chef d'oeuvre inconnu, Gambara, Massimila Doni.* Paris: Flammarion, 1981.
Barthes, Roland. *Le Degré zéro de l'écriture* (1953) et *Eléments de sémiologie* (1964). "Bibliothèque Médiations." Paris: Seuil, 1970.
Baudelaire, Charles. *Oeuvres complètes.* Ed. Marcel A. Ruff. Paris: Seuil, 1968.
Beaujour, Michel. "Short Epiphanies: Two Contextual Approaches to the French Prose Poem." In *The Prose Poem in France: Theory and Practice.* Eds. Mary Ann Caws and Hermine Riffaterre. New York: Columbia UP, 1983.
Beebee, Thomas O. "The Letter Killeth: The *Pli* of Death in Jean-Paul Marat's Epistolary Novel." *Clio: A Journal of Literature, History, and the Philosophy of History* 21,3 (1992): 217-241.
Benet, Robert. "Du regard de l'Autre dans les *Lettres persanes*: investigation, voilement, dévoilement." *L'Information Littéraire* 44,3 (1992): 6-13.
Bernard, Suzanne. *Le Poème en prose de Baudelaire jusqu'à nos jours.* Paris: Librairie Nizet, 1978.
Bessière, Jean, ed. *Figures féminines et roman.* Paris: PUF, 1982.
Blanchot, Maurice. *L'Espace littéraire.* Paris: Gallimard, 1955.
Boileau. *Art poétique.* Paris: Classiques Larousse, 1933.
Boren, Lynda S. *Eurydice Reclaimed: Language, Gender, and Voice in Henry James.* Ann Arbor, MI: UMI Research Press, 1989.
Borgerhoff, E.B.O. *The Freedom of French Classicism.* Princeton: Princeton UP, 1950.
Bray, Bernard and Isabelle Landy-Houillon, eds. *Lettres portugaises, Lettres d'une Péruvienne, et autres romans d'amour par lettres.* Paris: Flammarion, 1983.
Bronfen, Elisabeth. *Over Her Dead Body: Death, Femininity, and the Aesthetic.* New York: Routledge, 1992.
Buci-Glucksmann, Christine. *La Folie du voir: de l'esthétique baroque.* Paris: Editions Galilée, 1986.
Butler, Judith. *Gender Trouble: Feminism and the Subversion of Identity.* New York: Routledge, 1990.

Byatt, A.S. *Passions of the Mind*. New York: Vintage International, 1993.
Calasso, Roberto. *The Marriage of Cadmus and Harmony*. Trans. Tim Parks. New York: Vintage International, 1994.
Carrell, Susan Lee. *Le Soliloque de la passion féminine ou le dialogue illusoire*. Paris: Place, 1982.
Cassirer, Ernst. *The Philosophy of the Enlightenment*. Trans. Fritz C.A. Koelln and James P. Pettegrove. Princeton, NJ: Princeton UP, 1951.
Caws, Mary Ann and Hermine Riffaterre, eds. *The Prose Poem in France: Theory and Practice*. New York: Columbia UP, 1983.
Charpentier, Jeanne and Michel Charpentier, eds. *L'Encyclopédie ou dictionnaire raisonné des sciences, des arts et des métiers publié sous la direction de Denis Diderot*. Paris: Editions Bordas, 1967.
Charrière, Isabelle de. *Lettres de Mistress Henley publiées par son amie*. Eds. Joan Stewart and Philip Stewart. New York: MLA Texts and Translations, 1993.
———. *Oeuvres complètes*. Ed. Jean-Daniel Candaux, et al. 10 vols. Amsterdam: Van Oorschot, 1979-1984.
———. *Romans*. Paris: Le chemin vert, 1982.
Châtelet, Albert. *La Peinture française: XVIIIe siècle*. Geneva: Editions Skira, 1992.
Chauveau, Jean-Pierre. *Lire le baroque*. Paris: Dunod, 1997.
Chénier, André. *Oeuvres*. Paris: Gallimard, Bibl. de la Pléiade, 1966.
Chouillet, Jacques. *L'Esthétique des Lumières*. Paris: PUF, 1974.
Cixous, Hélène. "Le Rire de la Méduse." *L'Arc* (1975): 39-54.
Clouard, Henri and Robert Leggewie, eds. *Anthologie de la littérature française*. 2 vols. New York: Oxford UP, 1975.
Cook, Elizabeth Heckendorn. *Epistolary Bodies: Gender and Genre in the Eighteenth-Century Republic of Letters*. Stanford: Stanford UP, 1996.
———. "Going Public: The Letter and the Contract in *Fanni Butlerd*." *Eighteenth-Century Studies* 24,1 (1990): 21-45.
Condillac. *Traité des sensations; Traité des animaux*. Paris: Fayard, 1984.
Corneille. *Le Cid*. Paris: Classiques Larousse, 1970.
Coulet, Henri. *Le Roman jusqu'à la Révolution*. 2nd ed. Paris: Armand Colin, 1991.
Courtney, C.P. *Isabelle de Charrière (Belle de Zuylen): A Secondary Bibliography*. Oxford: Voltaire Foundation, 1982.
Cragg, Olga B. "Closure and the Doxa in the Feminine Novel of the Eighteenth Century in France." *Studies on Voltaire and the Eighteenth Century* vol. 304 (1992): 728-32.
Crosby, Emily A. *Une Romancière oubliée: Madame Riccoboni*. 1924. Geneva: Slatkine Reprints, 1970.
cummings, e.e. *100 Selected Poems*. New York: Grove Press, 1959.
Davison, Rosena. *Diderot et Galiani: étude d'une amitié philosophique*. *Studies on Voltaire and the Eighteenth Century* vol. 237. Oxford: Voltaire Foundation, 1985.
Deguise, Alix. "Mme de Charrière: Travel and Uprooting." *Eighteenth Century Life* 13,1 (1989): 42-48.
———. *Trois femmes; le monde de Madame de Charrière*. Geneva: Slatkine, 1981.
DeJean, Joan. *Ancients Against Moderns: Culture Wars and the Making of a Fin de Siècle*. Chicago: U of Chicago P, 1997.
———. "Looking Like a Woman: The Female Gaze in Sappho and Lafayette." *L'Esprit Créateur* 28,4 (1988): 34-45.
———. *Tender Geographies: Women and the Origins of the Novel in France*. New York: Columbia UP, 1991.
Demay, Andrée. *Marie-Jeanne Riccoboni ou de la pensée féministe chez une romancière du XVIIIe siècle*. Paris: La pensée universelle, 1977.
Deneys-Tunney, Anne. *Ecritures du corps de Descartes à Laclos*. Paris: PUF, 1992.

Diderot, Denis. *Encyclopédie.* Vol. 1. Eds. John Lough and Jacques Proust. Paris: Hermann, 1976.
———. *La Religieuse.* Paris: Flammarion, 1968.
Didier, Béatrice. *L'Ecriture-femme.* Paris: PUF, 1981.
Douthwaite, Julia V. *Exotic Women: Literary Heroines and Cultural Strategies in Ancien Régime France.* Philadelphia: U of Pennsylvania P, 1992.
Dowling, William C. *The Epistolary Moment: The Poetics of the Eighteenth-Century Verse Epistle.* Princeton: Princeton UP, 1991.
Eagleton, Mary, ed. *Feminist Literary Theory: A Reader.* Oxford: Basil Blackwell, 1986.
Eliot, T.S. *Collected Poems.* London: Faber and Faber, 1963.
Eymard, Julien. *Ophélie ou le narcissisme au féminin.* Paris: Minard, 1977.
Fauchery, Pierre. *La Destinée féminine dans le roman européen du dix-huitième siècle.* Paris: Armand Colin, 1972.
Fink, Beatrice. "Isabelle de Charrière: Correspondent, Novelist, and Woman of Independent Mind." *Eighteenth Century Life* 13,1 (1989): 1-3.
Freedman, Diane, Olivia Frey, and Frances Murphey Zauhar, eds. *The Intimate Critique: Autobiographical Literary Criticism.* Durham, NC: Duke UP, 1993.
Fried, Michael. *Absorption and Theatricality: Painting and Beholder in the Age of Diderot.* Chicago: U of Chicago P, 1988.
Gerson, Frédérick. *L'Amitié au XVIIIe siècle.* Paris: La pensée universelle, 1974.
Gevrey, Françoise. *L'Illusion et ses procédés: de 'La Princesse de Clèves' aux 'Illustres Françaises'.* Paris: Corti, 1988.
Gioanola, Elio. *Storia della letteratura italiana dalle origini ai nostri giorni.* Milan: Librex, 1987.
Girard, René. *Deceit, Desire, and the Novel: Self and Other in Literary Structure.* Trans. Yvonne Freccero. Baltimore: Johns Hopkins UP, 1965.
Goldsmith, Elizabeth and Dena Goodman, eds. *Going Public: Women and Publishing in Early Modern France.* Ithaca: Cornell UP, 1995.
———. *Writing the Female Voice.* Boston: Northeastern UP, 1989.
Goodden, Angelica. *The Complete Lover: Eros, Nature, and Artifice in the Eighteenth-Century French Novel.* Oxford: Clarendon, 1989.
Goodman, Dena. *The Republic of Letters: A Cultural History of the French Enlightenment.* Ithaca: Cornell UP, 1994.
Graffigny, Françoise de. *Lettres d'une Péruvienne.* New York: MLA Texts and Translations, 1993.
Grosz, Elizabeth. *Jacques Lacan: A Feminist Introduction.* New York: Routledge, 1990.
Hamilton, Edith. *Mythology.* Boston: Little Brown, 1942.
Harries, Elizabeth Wanning. *The Unfinished Manner: Essays on the Fragment in the Later Eighteenth Century.* Charlottesville: UP of Virginia, 1994.
Hassan, Ihab. *The Dismemberment of Orpheus: Toward a Postmodern Literature.* New York: Oxford UP, 1971.
Heilbrun, Carolyn G. *Writing a Woman's Life.* New York: Norton, 1988.
Herman, Jan. *Le Mensonge romanesque: paramètres pour l'étude du roman épistolaire en France.* Amsterdam: Editions Rodopi, 1989.
Herrnstein-Smith, Barbara. *Poetic Closure: A Study of How Poems End.* Chicago: U of Chicago P, 1968.
Hogarth, William. *The Analysis of Beauty.* New York: Garland Publishing, 1973.
Howells, R.J. "Désir et distance dans *La Nouvelle Héloïse.*" *Studies on Voltaire and the Eighteenth Century* vol. 230 (1985): 223-32.
Huet. *Traité de l'origine des romans.* Facsimile of 1670 edition. Stuttgart: Metzler, 1966.
Jacobson, Howard. *Ovid's Héroïdes.* Princeton: Princeton UP, 1974.

Janson, H.W. *History of Art*. Third ed. New York: Harry Abrams, 1986.
Jensen, Katharine Ann. *Writing Love: Letters, Women, and the Novel in France, 1605-1776*. Carbondale, IL: Southern Illinois UP, 1995.
Johnson, W.R. *The Idea of Lyric: Lyric Modes in Ancient and Modern Poetry*. Berkeley: U of California P, 1982.
Kamuf, Peggy. *Fictions of Feminine Desire: Disclosures of Héloïse*. Lincoln: U of Nebraska P, 1982.
———. "Seeing Through Rousseau." *L'Esprit Créateur* 28,4 (1988): 82-94.
Kavanaugh, Thomas M. *Esthetics of the Moment: Literature and Art in the French Enlightenment*. Philadelphia: U of Pennsylvania P, 1996.
Keats, John. *Complete Poems*. Ed. Jack Stillinger. Cambridge, MA: Harvard UP, 1982.
Kelly, Dorothy. *Telling Glances; Voyeurism in the French Novel*. New Brunswick, NJ: Rutgers UP, 1992.
Kristeva, Julia. *Histoires d'amour*. Paris: Denoël, 1982.
———. "La Femme, ce n'est jamais ça." *Tel Quel* (1974): 19-25.
Lacan, Jacques. *Le Séminaire, livre XI: Les quatre concepts fondamentaux de la psychanalyse*. Paris: Seuil, 1973.
Laclos, Pierre Choderlos de. *Les Liaisons dangereuses*. Paris: Flammarion, 1981.
Lacoue-Labarthe, Philippe and Jean-Luc Nancy. *L'Absolu littéraire*. Paris: Seuil, 1978.
Lacy, Margriet Bruyn. "Paradox in the Life and Works of Mme de Charrière." *Eighteenth Century Life* 13,1 (1989): 4-9.
Laden, Marie-Paule. "'Quel aimable et petit livre': Madame de Charrière's *Mistress Henley*." *French Forum* 11 (September 1986): 289-99.
Lafayette, Madame de. *La Princesse de Clèves*. Paris: Flammarion, 1966.
Lanser, Susan. "Courting Death: *Roman, romantisme*, and *Mistress Henley*'s Narrative Practices." *Eighteenth-Century Life* 13, n.s. 1 (February 1989): 49-59.
Lechte, John. "Woman and the Veil—or Rousseau's Fictive Body." *French Studies* 39,4 (1985): 423-41.
Levey, Michael. *Rococo to Revolution: Major Trends in Eighteenth-Century Painting*. New York: Thames and Hudson, 1992.
Lindsay, Jack. *Hogarth: His Art and His World*. London: Hart-Davis, MacGibbon, 1977.
Little, Roger. "Quelques poèmes en prose de Saint-Lambert." *Revue d'histoire littéraire de la France* 97,1 (1997): 113-18.
Locke, John. *An Essay Concerning Human Understanding*. 2 vols. London: J.M. Dent & Sons, 1961.
Lorris, Guillaume de and Jean de Meun. *Le Roman de la rose*. Ed. Daniel Poirion. Paris: Flammarion, 1974.
Loselle, Andrea. "Freud/Derrida as Fort/Da and the Repetitive Eponym." *MLN* 97,5 (1982): 1180-1185.
MacArthur, Elizabeth J. "Devious Narratives: Refusal of Closure in Two Eighteenth-Century Epistolary Novels." *Eighteenth-Century Studies* 21 (Fall 1987): 1-20.
Maclean, Ian. *Woman Triumphant: Feminism in French Literature, 1610-1652*. Oxford: Oxford UP, 1977.
Mallarmé, Stéphane. *Igitur, Divagations, Un coup de dés*. Paris: Gallimard, 1976.
———. *Poésies*. Paris: Gallimard, 1952.
Marivaux. *Le Jeu de l'amour et du hasard*. Paris: Classiques Larousse, 1990.
Marks, Elaine and Isabelle de Courtivron, eds. *New French Feminisms: An Anthology*. New York: Schocken Books, 1981.
Martinon, Philippe, ed. *Les Poésies de Malherbe*. Paris: Garnier Frères, 1926.
May, Georges. *Le Dilemme du roman au XVIIIe siècle: étude sur les rapports du roman et de la critique (1715-1761)*. Paris: PUF, 1963.
Merleau-Ponty, Maurice. *Le Visible et l'invisible*. Paris: Gallimard, 1964.

Miller, Nancy K. "The Exquisite Cadavers: Women in Eighteenth-Century Fiction." *Diacritics* (1975): 37-43.
Moi, Toril, ed. *French Feminist Thought: A Reader*. Oxford: Blackwell, 1987.
Molière. *Le Misanthrope*. Ed. G. Sablayrolles. Paris: Classiques Larousse, 1971.
Montesquieu. *Lettres persanes*. Paris: Flammarion, 1964.
Moser-Verrey, Monique. "Isabelle de Charrière en quête d'une meilleure entente." *Stanford French Review* 11,1 (Spring 1987): 63-76.
Mudge, Bradford. "Echo's Words, Echo's Body: Apostasy, Narcissism, and the Practice of History." *Tulsa Studies in Women's Literature* 10,2 (1991): 197-213.
Nietzsche, Friedrich. *The Birth of Tragedy*. New York: Penguin Books, 1993.
———. *The Will to Power*. Ed. Walter Kaufman. New York: Vintage, 1968.
Ogee, Frédéric. "Form and Fiction: Fielding and Hogarth's 'Line of Beauty'." *Studies on Voltaire and the Eighteenth Century* 264 (1989): 1077-1080.
O'Neal, John C. *The Authority of Experience: Sensationist Theory in the French Enlightenment*. University Park, PA: Penn State UP, 1996.
———. "Eighteenth-Century Female Protagonists and the Dialectics of Desire." *Eighteenth-Century Life* 10,2 (1986): 87-97.
———. "The Sensationist Aesthetics of the French Enlightenment." *L'Esprit Créateur* 28,4 (1988): 95-106.
Ostriker, Alicia. *Writing Like a Woman*. Ann Arbor, MI: U of Michigan P, 1983.
Ovid. *Heroïdes*. Trans. Henry T. Riley. London: George Bell & Sons, 1896.
———. *Metamorphoses*. Trans. Rolfe Humphries. Bloomington, IN: Indiana UP, 1957.
Pelckmans, Paul. "Le Rêve du voile dans *La Nouvelle Héloïse*." *Revue Romane* 17,1 (1982): 86-97.
Perry, Ruth. *Women, Letters, and the Novel*. New York: AMS Press, 1980.
Piau, Colette. "L'Ecriture féminine? A propos de Marie-Jeanne Riccoboni." *Dix-Huitième Siècle* 16 (1984): 369-85.
Preminger, Alex, ed. *The Princeton Handbook of Poetic Terms*. Rev. ed. Princeton, NJ: Princeton UP, 1986.
Quennell, Peter. *Hogarth's Progress*. New York: Viking Press, 1955.
Racine. *Phèdre*. Paris: Classiques Larousse, 1987.
Riccoboni, Marie-Jeanne. *Lettres de Milady Juliette Catesby à Milady Henriette Campley, son amie*. Paris: Desjonquères, 1983.
———. *Lettres de Mistress Fanni Butlerd*. Geneva: Droz, 1979.
Rice, Philip and Patricia Waugh, eds. *Modern Literary Theory: A Reader*. Second ed. Kent: Edward Arnold, 1992.
Rilke, Rainer Maria. *Sonnets to Orpheus*. Trans. David Young. Hanover, NH: UP of New England, 1987.
Rosbottom, Ronald C. "Narrating the Regency." *Romance Quarterly* 38,3 (1991): 341-353.
Roudat, Jean. *Poètes et grammairiens au XVIIIe siècle: Anthologie*. Paris: Gallimard, 1971.
Rougemont, Denis de. *Love in the Western World*. Trans. Montgomery Belgion. New York: Pantheon, 1956.
Rousseau, Jean-Jacques. *Emile, ou de l'éducation*. Paris: Flammarion, 1966.
———. *Julie, ou la nouvelle Héloïse*. Paris: Flammarion, 1967.
———. *Les Rêveries d'un promeneur solitaire*. Paris: Flammarion, 1964.
Rousset, Jean. *Forme et signification*. Paris: Corti, 1962.
———. *La Littérature de l'âge baroque en France: Circé et le paon*. Paris: José Corti, 1954.
———. *Leurs yeux se rencontrèrent: la scène de première vue dans le roman*. Paris: José Corti, 1981.
———. *Narcisse romancier: essai sur la première personne dans le roman*. Paris: José Corti, 1973.

Saint-Amand, Pierre. *Séduire, ou la passion des Lumières*. Paris: Méridiens Klincksieck, 1987.
Schneider, Pierre. *The World of Watteau: 1684-1721*. New York: Time-Life Books, 1967.
Segal, Naomi. *Narcissus and Echo: Women in the French récit*. New York: St. Martin's, 1988.
Sherman, Carol. "Diderot et la rhétorique du rococo." *Saggi e Ricerche di Letteratura Francese* 17 (1978): 249-273.
———. "Love's Rhetoric in *Lettres d'une Péruvienne*." *FLS* 19 (1992): 28-36.
———. "Passing Symmetry: Space and Time in Eighteenth-Century Esthetics." *Stanford French Review* 3 (1979): 223-233.
Showalter, English. *The Evolution of the French Novel: 1741-1782*. Princeton: Princeton UP, 1972.
Spencer, Samia I., ed. *French Women and the Age of Enlightenment*. Bloomington: Indiana UP, 1984.
Spitzer, Leo. "Les *Lettres portugaises*." *Romanische Forschungen* 65 (1954): 94-135.
Starobinski, Jean. *Jean-Jacques Rousseau: la Transparence et l'obstacle*. Paris: Gallimard, 1971.
———. "Les *Lettres écrites de Lausanne* de Madame de Charrière: inhibition psychique et interdit social." In *Roman et lumières au XVIII siècle*. Paris: Editions sociales, 1970. 130-151.
———. *Le Remède dans le mal*. Paris: Gallimard, 1989.
Stevens, Wallace. *The Collected Poems*. New York: Vintage Books, 1982.
Stewart, Joan Hinde. *Gynographs*. Lincoln, NE: U of Nebraska P, 1993.
———. "La Lettre et l'interdit." *Romanic Review* 80,4 (1989): 521-528.
———. *The Novels of Mme Riccoboni*. Chapel Hill, NC: North Carolina Studies in the Romance Languages and Literatures: Essays, vol. 8, 1976.
———. "Sex, Text, and Exchange: *Lettres neuchâteloises* and *Lettres de Milady Juliette Catesby*." *Eighteenth Century Life* 13,1 (1989): 60-68.
Strauss, Walter A. *Descent and Return: The Orphic Theme in Modern Literature*. Cambridge, MA: Harvard UP, 1971.
Swain, Virginia E. "Lumières et Vision: Reflections on Sight and Seeing in Seventeenth- and Eighteenth-Century France." *L'Esprit Créateur* 28,4 (1988): 5-16.
Sword, Helen. "Orpheus and Eurydice in the Twentieth Century: Lawrence, H.D., and the Poetics of the Turn." *Twentieth Century Literature* 35,4 (1989): 407-428.
Todd, Jane Marie. "The Veiled Woman in Freud's *Das Unheimliche*." *Signs* 11,3 (1986): 519-528.
Todd, Janet. *Women's Friendship in Literature*. New York: Columbia UP, 1980.
Todorov, Tzvetan. *Introduction à la littérature fantastique*. Paris: Seuil, 1970.
———. "Poetry Without Verse." In *The Prose Poem in France: Theory and Practice*. Eds. Mary Ann Caws and Hermine Riffaterre. New York: Columbia UP, 1983.
Tomlinson, Robert. *La Fête galante: Watteau et Marivaux*. Geneva: Droz, 1981.
Tompkins, Jane, ed. *Reader-Response Criticism from Formalism to Post-Structuralism*. Baltimore: Johns Hopkins UP, 1980.
Tong, Rosemarie. *Feminist Thought: A Comprehensive Introduction*. Boulder, CO: Westview Press, 1989.
Trousson, Raymond, ed. *Thèmes et figures du Siècle des Lumières: mélanges offerts à Roland Mortier*. Geneva: Droz, 1980.
Voisine, Jacques, ed. *La Poésie en prose des Lumières au Romantisme*. Paris: Imprimerie Claude Bernard, 1979.
West, Anthony, *Mortal Wounds*. London: Robson Books, 1975.
Wolf, Naomi. *Fire with Fire: The New Female Power and How it will Change the Twenty-first Century*. New York: Random House, 1993.

INDEX

absence, epistolary motif of, 13, 44, 137
Altman, Janet, 12, 15, 54, 61
anxiety of presence, concept of, 16-17

Balzac, Honoré de, 67
Baroque, French, 12, 103
Barthes, Roland, 34
Baudelaire, Charles, 74-79
beautiful death, Bronfen's concept of, 143
blank space
    and Lacanian unconscious, 63, 65
    and theatricality, 62
Boileau
    and French women writers, 13
    and history of French novel, 13, 35
brevity
    and epistolary writing, 15, 66, 78

Charrière, Isabelle de
    and narrative closure, 71
    and short text, 69
Classicism, French, 12, 32-34, 103
Condillac, 29-31
Corneille, Pierre
    concept of *gloire* in, 110-111
Crébillon fils, 89

death, as idea of perfection, 55, 64
déchirement, concept of, 138-145
DeJean, Joan
    and female gaze, 93-94
    and history of French novel, 13-15
desire
    and absence, 17
    and epistolary writing, 92

dévoilement, concept of, 138, 145
Diderot, Denis, 67, 106
différance, 79, 83, 137
disappearance of presence, concept of, 22, 135-136

écriture féminine, 82-83
epistolary lyric, 11, 17
epistolary writing, 34, 55
    as *poésie masquée*, 103
    as substitution for presence, 72
epistolary space, 48, 55
épistolière, 13, 71-72
Eurydice, 22, 155-156
evolution of French novel, 69

Fanni Butlerd
    and concept of *dévoilement*, 145
    and mourning, 99
    as writer, 89
Freud, melancholy and, 98-99

Gautier, Théophile, 67
gaze, 19, 93, 98
Graffigny, Isabelle de, 43, 46-48, 131
Guilleragues, 66, 74, 79

Hogarth, William, 123-126
    and serpentine line, 124
hors-scène, 54
    blank space as textual imprint of, 55-57
Huet
    and history of French novel, 67-68
Hugo, Victor, 19, 131

Lacan
   and fading, 134, 144
   and subject-object relations, 136
   and the gap, 62
   and unconscious, 63, 65
lack
   in relation to lyric, 17, 44
   in relation to woman, 19, 134
Laclos, Pierre Cholderlos de, 73, 123, 135
Lafayette, Madame de, 60, 97
letter-text, 57, 66, 103
Lettres persanes, 131, 134
Lettres portugaises, 66, 74, 79
Lettres de Milady Juliette Catesby, 109-114
Lettres de Mistress Fanni Butlerd, 81-82, 131
Lettres d'une Péruvienne, 45, 52-53
   theme of solitude in, 49
Locke, John, 29-30
Lorris, Guillaume de, 28
Lyric
   Derridean metaphor of, 24
   inability to define, 23
   peacock as metaphor of, 24
   Persephone as, 25

Malherbe, 29, 37
Mallarmé, Stéphane, 29-30
Marivaux, 33, 107
May, Georges, 34, 131-132
mediation
   concept of, 132
   veil as emblem of, 136
Montesquieu, 131
mourning
   and substitution, 99-100
   as epistolary theme, 100

Nietzsche, 23, 32

Ossian, 74

Persephone
   as allegory of Lyric, 22
   as allegory of mediation, 25, 31
   as figure of errancy, 22, 155
   as mark of absence, 25

portrait
   as substitution for presence, 93
   in *Fanni Butlerd*, 93-98
   in *La Nouvelle Héloïse*, 100
postclassical esthetic, 12, 65
presence, 82
   as epistolary motif, 93
prose poem, evolution of, 73-75

Racine, 36-39
Ricciboni, Marie-Jeanne
   and autobiography, 88
   and Italian theater, 109
rococo
   and epistolary writing, 103-106
Ronsard, Pierre, 28-29
rose
   as symbol of Lyric, 26-32
Rousseau, Jean-Jacques, 17, 57, 132, 138, 150
Rousset, Jean
   and *l'échange unilatéral*, 43-44

serpentine line, 122
   and epistolary narrative, 123, 126
short text, 66-71
silence, epistolary writing and, 54, 58, 81
solitude, 43, 49
Stevens, Wallace, 58

theatricality, 106-107
   and epistolary poetics, 115
Todorov, Tzvetan, 66
transparence, concept of, 33, 65, 139

veil
   and female body, 134-135
   as illusion, 138
   as mask, 64
   in relation to letter, 133-134
voilement
   in *Fanni Butlerd*, 145
   in *La Nouvelle Héloïse*, 138
Voltaire, 36-37

Watteau, 106, 110

NORTH CAROLINA STUDIES IN THE ROMANCE LANGUAGES AND LITERATURES

I.S.B.N. Prefix 0-8078-

Recent Titles

"EL ÁNGEL DEL HOGAR". GALDÓS AND THE IDEOLOGY OF DOMESTICITY IN SPAIN, by Bridget A. Aldaraca. 1991. (No. 239). *-9243-2.*
IN THE PRESENCE OF MYSTERY: MODERNIST FICTION AND THE OCCULT, by Howard M. Fraser. 1992. (No. 240). *-9244-0.*
THE NOBLE MERCHANT: PROBLEMS OF GENRE AND LINEAGE IN "HERVIS DE MES", by Catherine M. Jones. 1993. (No. 241). *-9245-9.*
JORGE LUIS BORGES AND HIS PREDECESSORS OR NOTES TOWARDS A MATERIALIST HISTORY OF LINGUISTIC IDEALISM, by Malcolm K. Read. 1993. (No. 242). *-9246-7.*
DISCOVERING THE COMIC IN "DON QUIXOTE", by Laura J. Gorfkle. 1993. (No. 243). *-9247-5.*
THE ARCHITECTURE OF IMAGERY IN ALBERTO MORAVIA'S FICTION, by Janice M. Kozma. 1993. (No. 244). *-9248-3.*
THE "LIBRO DE ALEXANDRE". MEDIEVAL EPIC AND SILVER LATIN, by Charles F. Fraker. 1993. (No. 245). *-9249-1.*
THE ROMANTIC IMAGINATION IN THE WORKS OF GUSTAVO ADOLFO BÉCQUER, by B. Brant Bynum. 1993. (No. 246). *-9250-5.*
MYSTIFICATION ET CRÉATIVITÉ DANS L'OEUVRE ROMANESQUE DE MARGUERITE YOURCENAR, par Beatrice Ness. 1994. (No. 247). *-9251-3.*
TEXT AS TOPOS IN RELIGIOUS LITERATURE OF THE SPANISH GOLDEN AGE, by M. Louise Salstad. 1995. (No. 248). *-9252-1.*
CALISTO'S DREAM AND THE CELESTINESQUE TRADITION: A REREADING OF *CELESTINA*, by Ricardo Castells. 1995. (No. 249). *-9253-X.*
THE ALLEGORICAL IMPULSE IN THE WORKS OF JULIEN GRACQ: HISTORY AS RHETORICAL ENACTMENT IN *LE RIVAGE DES SYRTES* AND *UN BALCON EN FORÊT*, by Carol J. Murphy. 1995. (No. 250). *-9254-8.*
VOID AND VOICE: QUESTIONING NARRATIVE CONVENTIONS IN ANDRÉ GIDE'S MAJOR FIRST-PERSON NARRATIVES, by Charles O'Keefe. 1996. (No. 251). *-9255-6.*
EL CÍRCULO Y LA FLECHA: PRINCIPIO Y FIN, TRIUNFO Y FRACASO DEL *PERSILES*, por Julio Baena. 1996. (No. 252). *-9256-4.*
EL TIEMPO Y LOS MÁRGENES. EUROPA COMO UTOPÍA Y COMO AMENAZA EN LA LITERATURA ESPAÑOLA, por Jesús Torrecilla. 1996. (No. 253). *-9257-2.*
THE AESTHETICS OF ARTIFICE: VILLIERS'S *L'EVE FUTURE*, by Marie Lathers. 1996. (No. 254). *-9254-8.*
DISLOCATIONS OF DESIRE: GENDER, IDENTITY, AND STRATEGY IN *LA REGENTA*, by Alison Sinclair. 1998. (No. 255). *-9259-9.*
THE POETICS OF INCONSTANCY, ETIENNE DURAND AND THE END OF RENAISSANCE VERSE, by Hoyt Rogers. 1998. (No. 256). *-9260-2.*
RONSARD'S CONTENTIOUS SISTERS: THE PARAGONE BETWEEN POETRY AND PAINTING IN THE WORKS OF PIERRE DE RONSARD, by Roberto E. Campo. 1998. (No. 257). *-9261-0.*
THE RAVISHMENT OF PERSEPHONE: EPISTOLARY LYRIC IN THE *SIÈCLE DES LUMIÈRES*, by Julia K. De Pree. 1998. (No. 258). *-9262-9.*

When ordering please cite the *ISBN Prefix* plus the last four digits for each title.

Send orders to: University of North Carolina Press
P.O. Box 2288
CB# 6215
Chapel Hill, NC 27515-2288
U.S.A.

www.ingramcontent.com/pod-product-compliance
Lightning Source LLC
Chambersburg PA
CBHW020741230426
43665CB00009B/510